TO MY POCKET

Fergusia, wife of George Lockhart of Carnwath.

"TO MY POCKET"

A personal Cash Book of an 18th Century Scottish Laird

Edited
by
S. F. Macdonald Lockhart

The Pentland Press
Edinburgh

First published by The Pentland Press
1984

ISBN 0 946270 09 0

Printed and bound by McCorquodale (Scotland) Ltd.
Jacket designed by Ann Ross Paterson

FOREWORD

George Lockhart of Carnwath lived for most of his life at Dryden House a few miles outside Edinburgh. It was there, for the most part, that he kept the meticulous record of his daily expenditure which is the subject of this book. The Cash Book did not however remain at Dryden. In 1789, James, or Jamie as he is frequently called, the Laird's surviving son, inherited the Estate of Lee and so became the Head of the Lockhart family as nineteenth Laird of Lee.

Coal mining is mentioned more than once in the Cash Book, and by the middle of the 19th century mining subsidence caused the family to abandon Dryden and about 1900 the house was demolished. Much more recently Carnwath House has also been pulled down to make way for a new Golf Club.

The Cash Book lay unnoticed for many years in the Lee Estate Office at Cartland, till in 1948 a new office was made of the stables at Carnwath and everything was transferred there. In 1976 a clearance was made in the loft above this office and a van was loaded with waste paper to be taken to the pulp mill. Something moved me to go through this load of rubbish. After more than 200 years the Cash Book was discovered. It was too late to include it in the Family History* which was by then in the hands of the printers. In any case this find clearly deserved a book to itself. Writing it has been a great adventure. Many gaps in my knowledge of the family, and of eighteenth century life, have been filled in. Only a very few of the entries are impossible to understand.

I have been helped by many people. The staff of the National Library of Scotland, where the Cash Book has at last found a permanent resting place, have shown unfailing willingness to help. To Dr. Alexander Fenton, Director of the National Museum of Antiquities of Scotland, I have turned whenever I found Scots words which I could not understand; I was never disappointed. Mrs. Winifred Alexander typed the final draft and Mrs. Annette Rose checked the proofs; to these and many others I offer my grateful thanks.

Dunsyre — Simon Macdonald Lockhart.
April, 1984

*Seven Centuries A History of the Lockharts of Lee and Carnwath. By Simon Macdonald Lockhart.

Dedication

For D. H. G.
With memories of C. classroom

INTRODUCTION PART I

THE LOCKHARTS OF CARNWATH

THE LOCKHARTS OF CARNWATH were a cadet of the Lockharts of Lee, being descended from George Lockhart, second son of James 13th Laird of Lee, and known as Lord Lee after his elevation to the post of Lord Justice Clerk. George followed his father's footsteps in a judicial career, and became President of the Court of Session, and one of the foremost lawyers of his time. He died at the hands of an assassin, a disgruntled litigant who shot him on his way home from church on Easter Sunday 1689.

The Lord President left two sons—George, the eldest, inherited the estates at the age of sixteen. He was a staunch supporter of the House of Stuart for whom he suffered both imprisonment and exile. He died in 1732 as the result of a duel. He was succeeded by his eldest son, another George, the author of the accounts which form the basis of this work. The younger son, Philip, was executed after the battle of Preston.

George Lockhart, the third Laird of Carnwath, married Fergusia Wishart, daughter of Sir George Wishart of Cliftonhall, from whom she brought a considerable dowry. George and Fergusia had a numerous family, eleven children actually growing up to adulthood. Several of these are mentioned in the accounts and deserve some description here. Like his father George was a Jacobite, and both he and his eldest son were at the battle of Prestonpans. This victory did not apparently impress the Laird as much as the poor quality and small numbers of Prince Charles Edward's supporters. He was evidently convinced that the probability of ultimate success was not great, and after the battle he rode with all speed to Dryden, his house near Edinburgh. Being a notable horseman he arrived there so quickly that he was able to convince General Cope, to whom he afterwards surrendered, that he had taken no part in the battle. As a result his estates were spared and he was merely exiled to Yorkshire for the duration of the Rising.

His eldest son, yet another George, marched with the Highland army, and became one of the Prince's Aides de Combat. After Culloden he went into exile with his Prince and died in Paris, without having been pardoned, in 1761. Thus he predeceased his father who died in 1764, and so the estates were saved from being forfeited, for had his father died first the eldest son would automatically have inherited, and as an unpardoned rebel his inheritance would have been seized by the Government. In fact the family went to great lengths to obtain indisputable proof of George's death, and save themselves from ruin. With the eldest son in exile the estates went to the second on their father's death in 1764; this was James, who had already had an adventurous and distinguished career. He was born in 1727. As a young man he chose a military career, and joined the army of Shah Nadir of Persia. This must have been before 1747, when the Shah fought a successful war against the Turks, being murdered soon after that. James probably went to Persia before the Rising of 1745; until his brother George had thrown in his lot with the Jacobites he can have had little expectation of inheriting his father's estates, and a career as a soldier of fortune would have been an exciting prospect for a young man.

After the death of the Shah, James moved back to Europe and became a soldier in the army of the Empress Queen Maria Theresa of Austria. He fought throughout the War of the Austrian Succession and won his way up from the lowest rank to that of General. He was created a Count of the Holy Roman Empire and a Lord of the Bedchamber. He was cited for bravery several times, and on one occasion was promoted to the rank of Senior Sergeant Major of Cavalry on the field by General Baron von Louden. On his father's death James took over the estates and brought his organising ability to bear on the running of them.

The eldest girl in the family was called Clementina, and she figures several times in the accounts; there is also quite a lot known about her from a collection of letters which she wrote to a friend, a Miss Mercer of Aldie. The main feature in Clementina's character must have been its strength; in the eighteenth century young ladies of her social standing did what their parents told them. In the field of matrimony especially 'Father knew best'. The marriage of any girl in a well-to-do family was an important political event; such alliances were made with other families in the same stratum of society with the object of strengthening the financial position of the family as well as making sure that the girl herself would have security. Political influence was of the greatest importance, particularly when young men sought employment, whether it might be in one of the services, in politics or diplomacy. To be able to turn to someone connected to the family who enjoyed the sort of power that could find a 'place' was almost vital in obtaining a start to a career. But Clementina, although she loved and respected her parents, would not accept their choice in the matter of a husband; in one of her letters she makes the pathetic comment, '. . . if ever I'm betrothed I don't expect (to) find a lover but surely I hope to have a friend in him which is all . . .'. In fact Clementina held out against her parents' numerous proposals until she was thirty-one years old. Then she married her childhood sweetheart, her cousin 'Jock' Gordon, who had been brought up with the Lockharts.

The only other girl in the family who is mentioned is Euphemia, and the accounts sadly record only her death and funeral expenses. She and Clementina were close friends and in her letters the elder sister tells her friend of the long illness and ultimate death of her 'friend and only sister' who had '. . . suffered those three days the most extreme continued pain as I would a slight headach(e) . . .'.

One other relation must be mentioned although there is only one entry in the accounts which may refer to him; William Lockhart, the Laird's younger brother. Will—as he is frequently called—served with Bligh's Regiment, the Twentieth of Foot, during the War of the Austrian Succession. He rose to be Adjutant of the Regiment, but as a Scot from a known Jacobite family in a Hanoverian Regiment he was never popular; after the battle of Fontenoy his brother officers accused him of cowardice, and he elected to stand trial by court-martial rather than resign his commission as his Colonel suggested. He was found guilty and cashiered. A cousin of the Lockharts, Frances Stuart, who held a high rank in the same army, wrote to the Laird saying in effect that Will had been framed, and had he not been a Scotsman with no senior officer to take up his case—Stuart himself was absent from the army and only returned two days after the court-martial—he would '. . . probably have a company in the same Regt. at this moment'.

Will made some effort to take service on the other side of the Atlantic, where knowledge of his disgrace might not have percolated, he may even have gone to America himself, as he was all prepared to go. He only awaited a passage, but whatever happened nothing came of the idea. He ended up on the Isle of Man, that haven of the destitute and the disgraced. There he found his brother Philip, the son whom his father had '. . . loved tenderlie . . .' and of whom he had expected so much. Alas, Philip had not turned out as his father had hoped; when Will joined him he was an alcoholic, and before many months had passed he died, largely as a result of his intemperance.

There is only one mention of Will in the accounts, but it may be an important one; during his self-imposed exile Will relied on brother George to look after his finances, which included the patrimony left him by his father. A disagreement arose between the two brothers over Will's allowance, and he was in danger of being arrested for debt. The entry in the accounts in the year 1763 records the dispatch of an express letter to the Isle of Man. George does not come out of this affair very well, but the brothers still remained on friendly terms. Will out-lived his brother and left the Isle of Man in his latter years.

After the Rising of 1745 it was difficult if not impossible for a Scotsman who had the reputation of being a Jacobite to obtain any post connected with the Government and there is no doubt where the Laird's political feelings lay. Murray of Broughton, a friend of the Lockharts, was Prince Charles Edward's Secretary of State throughout the Rising, but after Culloden he abandoned the cause and gave evidence against many of those who had been his former comrades. He refused however to implicate Lockhart of Carnwath, and stated that to the best of his knowledge he had never been introduced to the Prince. The remainder of his statement about the Laird is also interesting; in 1744 when it seemed certain that war between Britain and France was imminent Murray was engaged in collecting money, or promises of money, from those known to be in sympathy with the Stuart cause. He gave in his evidence a graphic picture of his interview with Lockhart of Carnwath;

'. . . I gave him to understand that it was not unlikely that something might soon be done in the King's (James) favour. This I did with a view to move his passions, raise his curiosity and draw such profession from him as might put it out of his power to refuse me. What I said seemed to have the desired effect, his face glowed with anxiety and his tongue was not wanting in the strongest expressions of zeal and attachment to the case . . .'. However when the question of a loan to King James was broached a marked change came over the Laird's attitude, '. . . but in place of an answer conform to the professions he had made, the joy which for some time had seated itself on his countenance immediately vanished and left nothing behind it but the gloom of disappointment. As soon as he had recovered a little he excused himself by saying that then was a most unlucky time, having no money by him and being obliged at Quarter Day to pay his brother's and sister's patrimonies . . .. I begged leave to observe that he had a Cash Account with the New Bank from which he could at any time draw a few hundred pounds . . .'. Lockhart prevaricated at this saying he had recently drawn a large sum from the bank and it might look odd and damage his future credit if he made another withdrawal so soon. Murray did everything in his power to persuade him, even offering to 'join his credit' with Lockhart's to give the impression that the money was a loan to him, but the Laird would only agree to consider the question and with this he had to be content. Although he raised the matter on several other occasions he could never persuade the Laird to make the loan.

In his Memorials Murray gives it as his opinion that Lockhart of Carnwath was so often asked for loans that he automatically refused. He concludes by saying that when the time came 'Carnwath acted with honour and spirit'.

There is no doubt that the Hunting Laird was a very rich man; the two estates of Carnwath and Dryden were on good land, and the process of improving them had been started at the end of the previous century by the Laird's father. The total rental from the estates must have been in the region of three thousand pounds per annum, and at a time when a day labourer received about twelve pounds a year and a skilled man like a gardener could be hired for under thirty pounds, this was great wealth. It must however be remembered that not all the rents were paid up; some are recorded as being 'desperate', in other words to be despaired of. Also, up to a quarter of the rents were paid in kind. Like many landowners then, as now, Carnwath may have often found himself short of cash.

It is of course quite possible that the Hunting Laird's father who was a dedicated and active Jacobite may have been too liberal in his contribution to the Stuart cause, and have landed the estate in heavy debt; there is no evidence of this, except that we know he did spend a great deal of money in his efforts to help his King. He raised a troop of horse from among his tenants and servants at Carnwath which had to be armed and horsed, clothed and paid. Finally after the defeat of the Jacobite army at Preston he bought many of the men their freedom when they had been condemned to transportation to the colonies as slaves.

The monetary system in Scotland was still in a primitive state in the eighteenth century; the Bank of Scotland was founded in 1695, and the Royal Bank of Scotland thirty years later. Even then the banking system could in no way be compared with that of today; in the Hunting Laird's personal accounts we shall find regular entries such as '. . . Pd the Royal Bank Servts. at clearing my Cash acct. with them—5/- . . .'. The Hunting Laird was a valued customer of the Royal Bank; the Minutes of the Court of Directors for August 7th 1752 read as follows:

> 'Read a letter from George Lockhart of Carnwath Esq. Proposing to borrow at Martinmas next Three thousand five hundred pounds sterling on Land or personal security, as should be most agreeable to the Bank and if on personal

> security The persons to engage with him would be unexceptional—Agreed to lend the above sum of three thousand five hundred pounds on personal Bonds, in regard Mr. Lockhart has been Serviceable to the Bank by bringing to the Office, the Specie he receive in payment of the Rents of his Estate from time to time . . .'.

The importance of this loan is illustrated by the fact that it was the second largest advance made by the Bank in that year; the largest being ten thousand pounds to the City of Edinburgh to finance the purchase of land for housing. Unfortunately we are not told the purpose for which Lockhart required this money. But clearly the Bank regarded him as a sound person to whom money might be advanced.

The Royal Bank of Scotland were not the only ones to believe that the Hunting Laird was a rich man. The lairds and aristocrats of the eighteenth century were continually in debt, and continually borrowing from Peter to pay off Paul. It would be tedious to list all the loans which are documented in family papers but there are some which merit a mention:

> '. . . Sir, I have this moment received the favour of your letter. I am really not so rich at present as to be able to send you that £50 you desire, but as soon as I receive any money which I hope will be in a very little time you shall command that or anything else in my power. I shall think myself very happy to see you and Mrs. Lockhart at Newliston. I am ever most perfectly
>
> Sir
>
> Your very obedt. Servant
>
> Stair.'

So even the Noble Earl of Stair was involved in financial trouble.

A letter from Charles Murray, one of the Broughton family, written in 1728 is even franker:

> '. . . I am drinking harder than I done since I saw you and must yrfore (therefore) beg your excuse for not writing so fully as both my duty and gratitude does oblige me. In the meantime however I must after returning you my hearty thanks for your last advise you of my draught of yesterdays date for £60 payable to Mr. Geo. Ochterlony or order against Whitsunday I shall by nixt post send you a promisory note for the value not knowing any person here that can draw a bond of relief.
>
> Etc. Charles Murray.'

At this time Murray was in such straitened circumstances that he did not dare to return to Scotland for fear of being arrested for debt.

In 1738 he asked Lockhart for a loan of twenty pounds, and was perfectly honest about the security of the money:

> '. . . it is obvious in the situation I am in that I cannot bid you rely on being suddenly repaid, to the contrary perhaps you never will, but if it please God I ever have it in my power, you may depend I will, and in the meantime will give you either bond or bill in what terms you shall please to direct me . . .'.

Another gentleman who had difficulty in paying his debts was Sir John Douglas of Kilhead in Dumfriesshire, but in his case the debt was not to Lockhart but to the Honourable Company of the Hunters of which Lockhart was the President. On February 11th 1754 Sir John wrote:

> '. . . All the world has been on my top this winter that I owed a shilling to, occasioned by Mr. Archibald Stuart my fellow sufferer leading an adjudication against me for £70 ode (odd) pounds. I made a great blunder about 12 months ago when I borrowed a sum of money to pay off my debts that I did not raise as much as to clear all demands. I have now negotiated a loan in England at 4 per cent to pay off every person at Whitsunday & make myself easy and independent. I had a summons execute before the Court of Session agst me about three weeks ago.. I desire you will give order that this affair be stopt & it shall all by payd at Whitsunday. I believe you know I do not want inclination to do justice to mankind & am losing no time in doing it . . .'.

Some days before writing this letter Sir John Douglas had been injudicious enough to write to a mutual friend of his and Lockhart's, Mr. William Maghie, who was also an office bearer in the Honourable Company, in terms very different to those he had used when addressing the Hunting Laird:

> 'Dear Willie,
>
> The Devile and every scoundrel I owe a farthing to are combined I believe to affront & harrass me with Diligence, & if they could would make me bankrupt, but thank God that is not in their power, the Great Mr. Lockhart of Carnwath is in the number of Drty Damnation Harpies . . . this great and mighty Nimrod is so complet a Dun and agent that he will not order . . .'.

Unfortunately the rest of the letter is illegible, but it is not hard to guess at the meaning. It was unfortunate for the writer that Mr.

Maghie showed this letter to Lockhart who kept it and wrote as follows to Sir John:

> '. . . this morning I went with Mr. Wauchope, Mr. Wright & Mr. St. Clair our Doctor to concert matters about our relief from the Hunters. Your letter was delivered to me directly and both Mr. Wauchope and I were most ready to stop the extracting any decreet agst. you, & to wait as you desired till Whity. for our payment . . . when you must pay off this debt . . . the cause is in the Session House but you will meet no further trouble. We ordered our agent to write to you on the head; after our business was over Mr. Maghie thought proper to hand me a letter you had writ him and desired me to read it, which I did and as it concerned myself pretty essentially I put it in my pocket, he asked it back & I told him he could not expect it since he had shown me the contents.
>
> You cannot imagine after 25 years of really friendship & the frankest intimacy &c &c after reading as kind a letter as ever I received from you how great was my surprise on reading the following words wrote & subscribed by you in your letter to Mr. Maghie. . .[1]. I own I must have seen it under your hand before I could have imagined you could have wrot so kindly to myself and in such a stile to any mortal man. I think it but fair to (tell) you I am in possession of your epistle to Mr. Maghie & your return to this shall regulate my future steps only depend on't I shall convince you that your old friendship was never placed unworthily. Few words are best in such affairs, I am etc . . .'.

This letter brought no reply from Sir John and on March 20th, Lockhart wrote again enclosing a copy of his original letter in case it had gone astray, and because he felt, '. . . I cannot express my sentiments nor the facts better than by Copying over the last letter I wrote you . . .'. This had the desired effect of convincing Sir John that he must make some sort of apology. The very mildness of Lockhart's attitude may have shamed him into replying. On March 24th he wrote from Kilhead:

> 'Sir,
>
> I received your letter . . . there are few men but on provocation are subject to passion and will boath in writing and speaking goe greater lengths than prudence & good manners allow. I do acknowledge that when I wrote to Mr. Maghie I was on my high horse & still think I was not well used. My case differ'd widely from any other of the Comp. of Hunters that refused to pay and are still debtors. I had paid the half and given a note for the Ballance so ought not to have been forced

throw the Court of Session. If Diligence had been done on my Bill it would not have vex'd me as the other matter did. I am contious to myself I never postponed any man's payment a hower (hour) when I could command the monie.

I do indeed aske your pardon for the expressions in my letter to Mr. Maghie I sollemly declare I neither minded the words nor the temper of mind I was in when I wrote them till I read your letter. But now since I have made acknowledgement to you I do insist that you write me a letter owning the summons sairved at your desire agst me was wrong and that you was sorry for it, when this is done I hope we are on the old footing of friendship which I shall always be desirous to maintain & I am &c &c.'

There is no further correspondence on this subject so it seems that the Hunting Laird accepted this rather half-hearted apology with the patience he had shown throughout the affair, which in other circumstances might have resulted in a duel. When money was owing between friends sordid little quarrels sprang up which could result in the death of one or both parties. The Hunting Laird kept his temper and refused to allow the matter to develop into a serious quarrel.

Long complicated lawsuits between families were quite common in the eighteenth century and the Lockharts were no exception. Indeed their particular case must be something of a record for it extended over forty years and by the time it was concluded both the original contestants had been dead for several years. A detailed account of the case, with all its appeals and cross appeals, has no place here but some aspects of it do illustrate the attitudes adopted by families when the ownership of land was in dispute. The case concerned the lands of Walston, at that time in the possession of the Baillie family.

Christopher Baillie of Walston died in 1694 leaving a substantial fortune to his son John, who was so improvident that he was soon known as Daft Baillie in Scotland and Mad Baillie in England. He neglected his family and estate without even appointing anyone to collect the rents; this naturally resulted in a considerable accumulation of debt. Although his personal fortune was ample to pay this off he became convinced that he was in danger of being sued for debts contracted in England, and retired into the Abbey of Holyrood which was at that time a sanctuary.

While he was in the Abbey Baillie was somehow persuaded that the only way out of his difficulties, which were actually not nearly as serious as he supposed, was to raise money on his estate of Walston. George Lockhart, the Hunting Laird's father, now appeared on the scene as a prospective purchaser. The case hinged on whether or not Baillie actually completed the sale to Lockhart, and if so whether it was an outright sale or merely a conveyance in the form of security. If the latter were the case, did Baillie have the right of re-purchase only at the end of twenty-one years or at any time during that period, and what was to be the purchase price? This was decided at twenty-one years purchase of the rental but so inefficient had Baillie's estate management been that the actual rental could not be established. Eventually the court declared that the rental in 1694 had been £4,792:11:0 Scots, equal to £399:7:7 sterling.

Baillie was declared 'fatuous and furious' in 1732 and died six years later in a mad house in Bethnal Green. The case was continued by his daughter, Grizel Rachel Baillie and her husband, Thomas Dickson; it was finally settled in Lockhart's favour by the House of Lords in 1748, and some of the lands of Walston still form part of the Carnwath Estate. It was what the Edinburgh lawyers would call a 'guid ganging plea'.

The legal fraternity were certainly the greatest beneficiaries of the system of continual indebtedness among the well-to-do. The ordinary loan of five or ten pounds could be dealt with by a simple bond or I.O.U. but when hundreds or even thousands of pounds were involved legal papers had to be drawn up. No doubt several copies had to be made, to say nothing of drafts, so the work of the clerks and apprentices who did the writing was considerable. One such among the family papers runs to twelve hand-written foolscap pages. This was a bond of provision by the Hunting Laird and his father, drawn up in 1721 when the Hunting Laird came of age, setting aside ten thousand pounds sterling to be divided between nine of the younger children.

Only the year before George Lockhart, second of Carnwath, had made over his whole estate to his eldest son. Just why he took this action we do not know. It may have been because he found himself in financial difficulties and thought that this was a way of saving the estate from his creditors, his son having married the daughter of a rich man. In fact, as soon as word went round that the transfer of the estate was planned, all the creditors came hurrying to demand the payment of their debts. It seems more likely that Lockhart, who was at this time acting as agent for the exiled King James, thought that in the event of his being discovered there was a serious danger of the estate being forfeited to the Crown and his numerous children left destitute. He may have hoped to avoid such ruin by transferring it to his son. His forebodings were justified, for in 1727 he barely escaped the Government troops and had to flee abroad. Such an action would have been typical of the man, whose loyalties were divided between his King and his family. The Hunting Laird made a similar decision after Prestonpans when he surrendered to General Cope, leaving his son to march with the Prince into eventual exile.

In 1756 a memorandum was submitted to the Hunting Laird on a claim made against him by Mr. James Hay for the sum of four thousand three hundred and twenty-eight pounds Scots. Hay was the executor for George Morrison, who had been factor on the estate from 1689 till his death in 1719. Hay claimed the repayment of the bond drawn in favour of Morrison by the Hunting Laird's father in 1718. The memorandum points out that thirty-seven years had elapsed since the bond was first drawn and no demand for payment had been made in that time although Morrison's children were in considerable need. Some of them having reached maturity had spent what fortune they had and were living on charity. If they were entitled to this money why had the matter not been raised earlier? We do not know the outcome of this case but it seems on first appearances that it was not very well founded.

There was also a loan made by Sir George Lockhart, the Hunting Laird's grandfather, to Lord Bargenny in 1688. The amount of the original loan was three thousand six hundred marks with two hundred marks penalty for non-payment of interest. For over sixty years the son and grandson of Sir George raised a succession of actions in attempts to recover this money. By 1721 the debt amounted to six thousand eight hundred pounds in spite of several substantial payments to account. By 1735 this amount had been reduced to one thousand seven hundred and nineteen pounds, but no further payments were made for the next fifteen years by which time the accumulated interest had brought the total up to three thousand and ninety-eight pounds. That is the last we know of the case but it is sufficient to show that a debt incurred by his grandfather was still a burden to the Hunting Laird many years later.

The last item in this description of the financial position of the family was indeed a family affair. Soon after the Rising of 1745, probably around 1748, the Hunting Laird granted a tack of his whole estate to his brother, Alexander, later Lord Covington. Why he took this action is not clear, but there can only have been one reason; he must have needed the money. The details of the tack are not known, but the result was that the income of the estate, about three thousand pounds a year, was divided between the two brothers. Possibly Alexander had paid a capital sum for his share and this money may have been what the Laird required. How he got into this difficulty has been suggested in the earlier part of this chapter.

The Hunting Laird died on December 24th 1764 at the age of 64, a good age for those days: attached to his Will is an inventory of the 'goods and gear' which were in his possession at the time of his death. This list tells us something of the way of life of a well-to-do family at that time. It should be remembered that the Laird had three houses, Dryden, the main home of the family, Carnwath (used mostly as a hunting lodge) and Bristow House in Edinburgh; all of these would be kept furnished and ready for guests.

(1)	199 dozen and 2 single table napkins, and 207 table cloths	£82–15– 0
(2)	196 pairs of blankets, 24 under blankets, 7 servitors[1], 58 feather beds, 65 feather bolsters, 91 pillows, 15 mattresses and 2 palliasses	£130–14– 6
(3)	65 bedsteads of different kinds with curtains window hangings bed covers &c and one small stool	£69– 8– 0
(4)	39 looking glasses of different sizes	£40–12– 0
(5)	4 curtains of chintz for a bed, with 3 window curtains of the same, one tester[2] curtain, 2 covers, 3 pawns[3], a white satin quilt and slip	No entry
(6)	One white mareil calico quilt, 3 pillow cases and 2 white window curtains, and 115 yards of material for blankets.	£13–19– 0
(7)	12 spindles of yarn, 4 spindles of cotton and 35 pounds of lint	£1–13– 6
(8)	6 settees and 168 chairs of different kinds	£54–19– 6
(9)	44 pieces of carpet large and small	£17– 8– 6
(10)	92 tables of different kinds	£35–15–10
(11)	16 Screens large & small of different kinds	£16– 4– 0
(12)	31 chests of drawers of different kinds	£10–12– 2
(13)	29 Chests trunks and presses for different uses and different kinds	£9– 2– 0
(14)	2 fir chests, four mahogany boards, 1 tea tray, 2 pairs mahogany stands, 2 pair mahogany candle sticks, 1 large harpsicord with 1 case, 2 large chests, 4 chests of drawers, 3 fir presses, 1 cupboard, 1 calton wheel and reel	£11– 5– 0

(15)	11 cason standards[4] of different kinds	£0–16– 0
(16)	13 water pots	£1–17– 3
(17)	A yellow cover & cashion, 1 window curtain, 3 hangings, 1 mattress for a bunker, 1 lamp & pelt[5], 1 basket brass hooped, 1 marble mortar & pistol[6], 1 brass do, 1 pair scales, 4 bird cages, 4 shagreen cases, 3 baskets, 4 bottle salvers, 6 bonnets, 2 kitchen tables, hens cribs, salt chests, one tent for sewing[7], one mangle and screen, 2 baskets, 6 wheels, 2 paks of cards, 1 check reel, 1 large glass globe, 2 rubbers & hair besoms. 1 long pole & strap, 5 candle boxes, & broken chairs, 2 trunks, 1 stand for a tea kettle, 5 basin stands, 2 mahogany do. & do. for paris plaster, 2 large lustres [8] with branches, and 4 tea boards	£9 1 6
(18)	An old spinet, 3 wheels & 2 reels[9], 1 pair windles & 2 tea chests, 1 basket brass-hooped, a parots cage, 4 small mahogany boards, & 5 bonnets, 3 baskets, 1 plate warmer, 3 lamps for passages, 1 tent for the door, 2 candlesticks, 1 bunker, 1 crib, 1 washing rubber. 1 long pole besom, 6 hearth besoms[10], 4 jappaned candlesticks, 3 sole do. with extinguishers, 1 glassed map with frame, 2 Mahogany candlesticks, 1 candle stand, 1 bagammon table, 1 warming pan	£4 0 9
(19)	9 earthen cans, 1 milk pail, 1 churning barrel, 1 sieve, 1 butter print, 1 screen, 1 table, 1 churning barrel, 6 milk cogs[11], 2 caps & 2 tables.	£0 14 6
(20)	5 Clocks with clock cases of different kinds	£11 11 0
(21)	56 chimneys[12], 18 fenders, 29 pokers & 42 pairs of tongs of different kinds	£25 0 7
(22)	China of all kinds	£20 0 6
(23)	Chrystal & glasses of different kinds	£7 5 3

(24)	Silver Plate weighing 1454 ounces 13 dropes	£375 16 6¼
(25)	The pictures and prints	£79 3 0
(26)	The copper brass and pewter	£42 19 10
(27)	The iron furniture	£1 2 7
(28)	The brewing looms & cellar furniture	£14 2 10
(29)	All sterling money £1169–15–7 and after deducting £398–18–65/12 being the value to which Fergusia had right by contract of marriage there remains	£770 17 05/6
(30)	The books in the defuncts library	£150 0 0
(31)	The corn hay horses & farming utensils, cattle & stable furniture at Dryden	£284– 1– 0
(32)	The Ditto at Carnwath	£203– 7– 4
(33)	The garden tools	£27–19– 1
(34)	A coach, phaeton postchaise, and 2 wheeled chaise	£37–10– 0
(35)	The coach, hunters & saddle horses	£125–12– 6
(36)	Total after deducting £1608–15–115/6	£19306– 3–10

(37) Debts owing:—

1. £13150–1–7 Scots=½ yrs money rent from Martinmas 1763 to Whits 1764 payable by tenants in Clydesdale.
2. £1198–7–10 Scots. feu & teind duties
3. £2298–7–6 payable by Dryden tenants
4. £408–18–0 parks etc. rents
5. £971–1–8 tenants of Old Liston
6. £2785–5–6 meal rent from Clydesdale

(38) Total=£20,818–17–8 Scots being £1734–17–8 Stg. less £168–6–0 ½ years stipend etc.

(39) Free rental £1562–11–8 Stg.

(40) Also owing by J. Stodart the Girnel keepers £286–12–5=£1853–12–5 Stg. or £22,238.9.0. Scots.

Notes on the inventory

At first sight it is almost unbelievable that any household should require 2390 table napkins: however if we consider that there were three houses and each one might have to be able to entertain 20 guests for perhaps a week, and that each guest might use 2 or even 3 napkins per day the quantity does not look quite so impossible. All laundering would be done at home without the help of washing machines, tumble dryers or even constant hot water, so there would have to be enough linen to keep the household equipped until the dirty napkins were washed and dried and ironed. A week might not be any too long in bad weather. There would also be 'best' linen and everyday; there may have also been napkins for the upper servants. These remarks apply to several of the other entries in the inventory also. The scale of housekeeping in a large eighteenth-century house was really enormous by today's standards; apart from anything else the number of servants who had to be clothed, fed and housed must have created a great amount of work.

Notes on Inventory attached to the Laird's Will

1. Servitors—table napkins or hand towels.
2. A tester was the canopy over a four poster bed.
3. Pawns were narrow curtains fixed to the bottom of a bed.
4. Cason standards are probably uprights for supporting or the framing for a chest.
5. A pelt—perhaps some sort of lampshade.
6. Pistol—presumably pestle.
7. A tent for sewing is a stretching frame commonly used for embroidery or tapestry.
8. Lustres were Chandeliers.
9. Wheels cards and check reel probably all connected with spinning.
10. Besoms—brushes.
11. A milk cog was a wooden basin for holding milk.
12. 56 chimneys; perhaps we would have called them fireplaces.
13. The most notable omission from the inventory is the kitchen equipment, nor is there any mention of knives or spoons. They may be included in the 1454 ounces 13 dropes of silver plate, but surely there must have been something for the servants to eat with?

Note on Part I of the Introduction

1. Here followed a copy of Sir John Douglas' original letter.

INTRODUCTION PART II

THE CASH BOOK

Considering its age the Cash Book is in excellent condition; it is written in a hard covered book measuring 375 mm. by 250 mm. The Laird's handwriting is bold and clear and only in a few places is the text marred by erasures. It cannot be said, however, that he was accurate in his addition. There are several mistakes, and it does not seem that the totals were ever checked; this however does not diminish the value of the book as a record of how the Scots upper class lived in the eighteenth century.

The entries in the book are divided into nine headings: To My Wife; To My Pocket; To Our Cloaths; To My Stables; Laboring & Miscellanys; Servts Wadges and Livery; Plate Meal Malt Etc; To My Children; My House in Edinr.

The Cash Book covers the period from 1728 to 1764, the year the Laird died, but only the last five years are given in detail in this book. The previous years are given in the form of a summary.

To My Wife

Fergusia Wishart of Cliftonhall near Edinburgh married George Lockhart in 1726. On her depended the efficient management of the households at Dryden, Carnwath and Bristow House in Edinburgh, and for this purpose her husband supplied her with money at an average rate of £469 per year. Out of this she had to pay all the female servants—the Laird paid the male staff—and purchase all the food required by the establishment. It is not clear how many female servants there were at Dryden; then, as now, extra hands were probably taken on when the house was full. Lady Grizel Baillie in her House Book records 17 servants at Mellerstain both male and female; she also gives the following rates of pay:

Butler	£14	per year
Footman	£5	,, ,,
Coachman	£8	,, ,,
Groom	£2.10.0	,, ,,
Postillion	£2	,, ,,
Carter	£4	,, ,,
Gardener	£14	,, ,,
Housekeeper	£5	,, ,,
Ladysmaid	£5	,, ,,

Cook	£8	per year
Under Cook	£3	,, ,,
Kitchen Maid	£2	,, ,,
Chambermaid	£2	,, ,,
Laundrymaid	£2	,, ,,
Dairymaid	£2	,, ,,
Herd without Meat	£5	,, ,,
Officer ,, ,,	£7.5.0.	,, ,,

Apart from their wages and food the servants had to be decently clothed, as also had the family. Their clothes must have made a considerable demand on the housekeeping money until they reached an age when they received an allowance from the Laird and did their own shopping.

Most of the entries in this section are quite straightforward, 'To My Wife' or occasionally to 'My Wife for our Children'. When the Laird was ill in London and Fergusia went south to look after him there was a variation, 'To my Wife when in London with me—£290'. And 'Pd my Wife's journey to London by £50 taken from the Bank and now repayd—£50'. There are also some special payments to Fergusia for the purchase of furniture for Bristow House when it was bought as a town house in Edinburgh.

Over the thirty-six years covered by the Cash Book the Laird paid to his wife the large sum of sixteen thousand eight hundred and eighty-eight pounds; this was 23.3% of his total expenditure and the second highest amount under any of the headings. It was exceeded only by the seventeen thousand one hundred and fifty-two pounds paid out 'To My Children'.

To My Pocket

This heading is sometimes called simply 'Pocket Money' and it includes all kinds of personal expenses which were not covered by any of the other sections. In fact the Laird put into this section several items which might have been included elsewhere in the accounts. There are, for instance, regular entries referring to payments made to the livery servants. Some of these are refunds of money spent by them on their master's behalf for such things as tolls on the roads, the purchase of fallen sheep and horses for hound food and other small commissions, but the frequent mention of board wages might surely have been put in the section concerned with servants' wages and livery. It seems that for some reason the Laird wished to keep the ordinary wages and clothing of his servants separate.

George Lockhart was an enthusiastic follower of the chase and also a racing man. Expenditure on both these pursuits is entered in this section although his hunters and race horses were fed and stabled along with the other horses belonging to the family. When they had special diets or went away to race meetings or hunts these extra expenses are kept in here. Horse racing immediately suggests betting and the Laird was certainly not averse to backing his own horses. He must have been either very successful or only put money on his horses when he was sure they were going to win because there are only two instances of his having to pay out lost bets; those that he won would not appear in the Cash Book, but one of the first entries in the book is: 'Pd. to Mr. Murray my beat lost at Kelso by Lord Aboyne turning without a post........£42.' Lord Aboyne was the Laird's nephew; his sister Grace had married the Earl of Aboyne, and on his death the Earl of Moray. The children of the first marriage were brought up with the Lockharts, and the Laird's eldest daughter Clementina married her cousin Jock Gordon, a brother of the Earl mentioned here. Going off course and so losing the large sum of forty-two pounds for his uncle cannot have been popular.

Apart from the frequent entries about money spent by the servants, and racing and hunting expenses, 'Pocket Money' covers a wide range of personal outgoings, varying from twenty-four pounds seven and five pence for the funeral of the Laird's second daughter Euphemia to six shillings paid for a pound of tea given to a Mrs. Kerr as a present.

The health of the family comes under this section. In 1758 Fergusia must have been quite ill; she had two visits from Dr. Clerk at two guineas a time, and was blooded twice by Mr. Rattray and once by Dr. Gibson who also applied a blister for which he only charged one guinea. Mr. Rattray may have been the surgeon of that name who had married the Laird's youngest sister Mary.

While he was in London during the winter of 1758–59 the Laird was taken ill and tended by his valet William McKye and his landlady and her husband Mr. and Mrs. Finlayson. He was attended by Dr. Pringle whose bill was sixteen guineas; Mr. Forbes got a guinea for bleeding the Laird twice. There was also an account for six pounds sixteen shillings and six pence for drugs; William McKye received a guinea for looking after the Laird while he was in a fever, as well as his expenses for housekeeping, washing and other outgoings, including asses' milk for the invalid. While he was away Fergusia kept an account of all payments made by her, and when she came down to London to be with her husband James Stodart the factor kept the accounts, both changes being recorded by marginal notes made by the Laird.

This was the Laird's second journey south within a few weeks; in September 1758 William Kelly the coachman drove his employer to Cambridge, from where the Laird continued his journey to London to obtain a licence to travel abroad. He went on to Harwich and crossed to Rotterdam; and the total cost of this journey and the return to Dryden came to one hundred and sixty-five pounds six shillings and ten pence, excluding the six pounds eleven shillings and ten pence for William Kelly's expenses taking the coach and horses back from Cambridge to Dryden. We are not told the reason for the Laird's lightning visit to the Low Countries—he was back home within six weeks for he set out again for London at the end of October. One explanation may be that he went to visit his eldest son, James, who as we have already mentioned had been in exile in France since the collapse of the Jacobite Rising in 1745.

Charity and gifts of all kinds come under this heading: 'To my Nurse in Charity ten shillings . . . Dinner and musick to my coaliers on my birthday £1–6–0 . . .'. And when his horse Spot won a race, in which no doubt he had backed him heavily '. . . drinks to Carnwath people on Spots victory £1–6–0'. Two flannel waistcoats for the factor and a pair of silver knee and shoe buckles for the gardener as well as collections for the infirmary and many other such entries over and above the regular payments for the poor in the parishes of Liberton and Carnwath indicate that the Laird was a generous man.

To Our Cloaths

The next section shows that if the Laird was a generous man he certainly was not an extravagant one; his expenditure on clothes amounted over the whole period of thirty-six years to two thousand nine hundred and twenty-three pounds. This was only 4% of the total expenditure in that time. It is noticeable in the first three of the six-year periods the rate is much higher than in the last three, more than double in fact; this is understandable. A young man, newly married and moving in a fashionable society would spend more on his appearance than an older man, who in any case would have acquired a stock of clothes many of which while old and out of fashion might still be serviceable.

Individual items purchased under this heading are varied, '2 fine hats, 3 pair white silk stockings . . . 6–5–0, 4 bob wigs at a pound a piece', are typical entries. The Laird was economical in having his clothes repaired when they showed signs of wear rather than discarding them and buying new ones; the entry 'for dressing & a new lace to ane old hat' occurs twice in September and October 1758, the cost being six shillings and eight pence the first time and seven shillings and two pence the second. There are other similar entries.

This section also covers items bought for Fergusia and the children: these are usually lumped together and not itemised; in 1761 he paid a large bill to Mr. Hope, fifty-nine pounds for articles supplied to the family, and in the next year he paid the same person seventy-seven pounds for clothes for himself and his wife. Even in the year before he died the Laird was renewing his wardrobe and paid two bills for clothes to be worn at the meetings of the Honourable Company of Hunters. But in the following year the only entry is for two bob wigs and other trifles bought from Thomson's widow.

To My Stables, Horses, Coach and Hounds Etc is the next section, and it is a large one amounting to 11.6% of the total expenditure and coming third after 'My Children' and 'My Wife'. This is quite understandable when it is remembered that the stables were the transport division for the whole estate; here were kept the riding horses for the family as well as their coach horses and also the cobs and hacks which were ridden by the grooms and other servants on errands in the district. It must be remembered too that the estate was a large one and to send a message from Dryden to Carnwath and back, which must have been a frequent occurrence, involved a journey of forty-five miles. In addition there would have been the draught horses which did all the haulage on the estate; this would include the transport of the grain and meal, paid as part of the farm rents, from the girnels at Carnwath and Symington to Dryden or wherever else it was required for the consumption of the family or the payment of the servants.

Food for the Laird's horses and hounds provided a valuable outlet for the farmers on the estate for the sale of hay, straw and grain, as well as consuming quantities of offal from the slaughter houses. This is illustrated by such entries as:

'Pd John Paterson for 20 bolls of meal laid up at Carnwath 15.0.0'. Paterson was a large supplier to the Laird and in the same year (1758) he sold straw and corn to him to the value of eighty-eight pounds. In the following year the tenants at Carnwath and Dryden supplied straw, corn and fodder to the amount of nearly a hundred pounds. Farmers by the name of Cochrane and Weir regularly supplied their hay crop at a price of about forty pounds

Extends 96 Feet

The West Front of Dryden House towards the Court the Seat of George Lockhart of Carnwath Esqr.
in the County of Midd-Lothian.

Gull & Adam delin *R. Cooper Sculp*

which must have been a useful addition to their budget. The blacksmith was a monthly visitor to both Carnwath and Dryden and there were bills from the saddler, and the veterinary expenses to settle too. The stables and kennels made a useful contribution to the economy of the estate.

Discharge on Labouring, Building, Ditching, Books & all other Miscellanys is a very comprehensive heading. The inclusion of Books seems strange as the other items are all related and might have been called 'Farming & Estate Work' or some similar title. There are only three books mentioned in the whole period and these could have been listed much more suitably under Pocket Money. However for some reason unknown to us the Laird included them in this section. The very first entry in January 1758 reads 'Pd. Mr. Gordon for a new acc^{t} book 11.0.' This is almost certainly the actual book with which we have been concerned throughout these pages. The other books bought were 'A large Bible for myself' costing a guinea, also in 1758, and in the following year, '4 vollums of Lidia' at twelve shillings.

The total amount of money spent under this section during the thirty years was seven thousand seven hundred and fifty-seven pounds, an average of two hundred and fifteen pounds per annum, and 10.6% of the total expenditure. The annual range is not great varying from £356 in 1732 to £87 in 1730.

The section covers all kinds of farm and estate work including the gardens, which were of some importance employing a gardener and three lads at Dryden; they got nine pounds between them which was raised to eleven pounds in 1763. Moles were a pest then as now, and the gardener received an extra payment for killing them; birds were kept off the fruit trees with nets. Improvements to the gardens included the planting of nine beech trees; these must have been large specimens, instant trees we would call them today, as a number of men were hired for twelve shillings and six pence to transport them to the 'garding'. The Laird also had twelve orange trees in his garden which were kept in iron tubs. The gardener was responsible for raising young trees for planting out in the woods, and also hedging plants for enclosing fields; he was probably the most highly trained man on the estate.

The bulk of the expenditure went on wages, both meal and money, of the 'work servants', that is the outdoor servants who worked the land, maintained the buildings, and felled the trees in the woods which were mainly used for repairing the estate houses and other buildings: 'Pd James Monylas for sawing deals and couples' and even more specifically: 'for sawing deals and couples for tenants houses'. This indicates a decline in an old custom whereby each tenant owned the 'roof-tree' of his house. When he moved at the end of his tenancy the thatch was stripped off and thrown on the midden and the man carried away with him the main beam which supported the roof to erect it on his next dwelling.

The Laird's grandfather had been one of the first to start enclosing and improving his estate in the latter part of the seventeenth century, and the process was still being continued fifty years later. The old run-rig system by which each holding was divided up into a number of narrow strips scattered over the township prevented any form of improvement; by enclosing the farms into contiguous fields more food was produced and stock could be over-wintered and grown to a size which was not possible under the old system. There are several mentions of ditching and planting hedges with 'quighs' or thorns from the gardens, as well as two definite mentions of farms being enclosed, both in 1762:

> 'Jayr 30. Pd for enclosing William Murrays farm at Dryden £5.3.0.
> Feby. 28 Pd for enclosing Widdow Ainsleys farm at Dryden £4.9.3.'

There are also several mentions of the formation of new parks at Carnwath—there is still a farm just outside the village called 'The Park'—and this entailed a considerable amount of work. We read in 1762:

'Pd for Dung gathering stones, cutting rashes, filling dung, spreading &c about Carnwath new park £6.8.3'.

And again in the following year:

'Andrew Somerville and 4 other men for filling up peet holes, and making water runs in Carnwath parks £3.19.0'.

The last entry gives an indication of the amount of trouble that was taken to form a good field. The land round Carnwath is much glaciated and there are pockets of peat in among the sandy soil left by the glaciers; these pockets form wet holes which greatly interfere with agricultural work unless they have been filled in with mineral soil. Andrew Somerville and his four companions must first have dug out the peat—perhaps it was taken for fuel—and then carted in soil to fill up the resulting holes. Drainage by underground tiles was still unknown so that ditches had to be dug to run off the surface water from the new fields.

The heating and cooking of food in the mansion houses of Carnwath and Dryden needed large quantities of fuel. Wood, coal and peat were all used for this purpose; the coal came from the Laird's coal mine at Dryden, where there are still mines, the wood was cut in the plantations, and the peat was won in the Carnwath peat moss, where the old peat road which was used for bringing fuel into the village may still be seen. In 1762 over six hundred loads of coal were carted to Carnwath house; this appears to be a very large amount but it must be remembered that the loads would have been very small, perhaps only a few hundredweight each, to be dragged over the rough roads by horses. We are not told from where the coal was brought; if from Dryden it was a long haul. More likely it came from one of the mines in the north of Lanarkshire.

The last item of note in this section is the digging of clay for brick-making at Carnwath. This is another indication of the building work that was going on on the estate, and it must have been important. As has already been mentioned the land round Carnwath is almost entirely sand and gravel and some considerable search must have been made to find a seam of clay. This entry also indicates the difficulty of transporting a heavy material in large quantities even over comparatively short distances; clay was readily available ten miles away on the Lee estate belonging to another branch of the Lockhart family, where there has been large-scale brick-making for many years.

Servants Wadges and Livery took up only three thousand two hundred and thirty-five pounds, or 4.4% of the total outgoings in the thirty-five years covered by the accounts. From this two things suggest themselves; first that wages were extremely low when compared with other items, and secondly that, when taken in conjunction with the 4.0% spent on clothes the Lockharts were neither extravagant nor self-indulgent.

The servants to whom this section refers were the male liveried servants who worked in the house and stables; footmen and grooms, mostly, with some senior men in each department. They wore the Laird's livery and were also supplied with 'frocks', or overalls made from ticking called Gallashields cloth, to protect their uniforms when doing dirty work such as cleaning boots and grooming horses. On one occasion the footman William MacKye received a guinea as compensation for wearing his own 'frock'. It was important for the prestige of the family and the morale of the servants that they should be smartly turned out when guests came to the house or when they went riding out either with their master, or alone taking messages to neighbouring houses.

The servants were paid half yearly, at Whitsun and Martinmas, a system which continued into the twentieth century on some estates, and one which could give rise to hardship. There are frequent records of men being given advances of pay between the two statutory pay-days. The wages paid to the livery servants ranged from three or four pounds per year up to six or seven for the senior ones. In addition they got their board and lodging, and no doubt they fed better and slept more comfortably than their brothers who remained on the farms. There was a fair turnover among the grooms and footmen, with men leaving and others being taken on, but only one instance of a man being dismissed—for insolence.

Plate, Meall, Malt and Wine is a section which should tell us something of the manner in which the Lockharts lived; a total expenditure of almost six thousand pounds in thirty-five years gives an annual average of one hundred and seventy-one pounds, or 8.1% of the total expenditure. We may straight away dispose of 'Plate'; the only entry referring to this is an annual entry of two pounds and fifteen shillings as 'plate duty'. The remaining items come out at the following proportions: meal 26%; malt 9%; ale 12%; rum 8%; wine 42%; other 3%.

From this it is clear that the Laird kept a good cellar, and spent quite large sums of money on replenishing it. Wine would have made a daily appearance on his table for the family and their guests. Ale would have been available in the servants' hall, but above stairs claret and madeira were served, having been imported in bulk and bottled at home. One unusual entry is in March 1760; 'Pd Lord Errol in full for Mountain wine he sent me £5.10/-'. 'Whiskie' is only mentioned once though rum seems to have been popular, often drunk as punch. There is nothing in the accounts to suggest excessive drinking, only the kind of good living that was in keeping with the time. We may compare the amount of wine bought by the Laird with the actual consumption recorded in the cellar book from Lee covering the period from December 6th 1825 to April 30th 1826. In this period of twenty weeks including Christmas and New Year, when there would be entertaining and celebration, the household drank 200 bottles of port, 257 of sherry and 12 other undecipherables; the Christmas and New Year festivities accounted for 35 Port, 15 Madeira, 24 Sherry, 2 Claret and 2 Brandy. At this time the Laird of Lee was Charles Macdonald Lockhart, great-grandson of the Laird with whom we are concerned, and a gentleman not renowned for his temperate habits.

To my Sons at School, or To my Children is the last but one regular entry in the accounts. It first appears in 1738, when George the eldest son was twelve years old, and the birth of Charles the youngest was still two years away. The total cost to the Laird of educating his family was seventeen thousand one hundred and fifty-two pounds, and this comes out at almost 25% of his total expenditure. Education was a heavy burden on parents.

To my House Rent in Edinburgh is the last of the regular entries in the Laird's accounts; it first appears in 1738 and continues until the year of the Laird's death. The sum runs steadily at fifty pounds a year except for the years 1745 and 1746, and 1748 and 1749. Both pairs of years are lumped together; in the first case the rent is three times the former annual rent, and in the second case it is given as seventy pounds instead of one hundred as would be expected. In each case the rent reverts to the ordinary amount of fifty pounds in the following year.

In 1761 there is a change in the arrangement. The Laird bought a house in Bristow Street—a continuation of what is now King George IV Bridge and no longer standing—from the architect John Adam. The house had been called Ross House but the Laird renamed it Bristow House. The purchase included 20 acres of land, a large area to buy within the City boundaries, and was part of Heriot's Cross and the Windmill acre. The purchase price is not known, but the transaction was a complicated one as the seller retained a feu duty of ten pounds a year over the subjects and there were dues to be paid to the Magistrates and other officials of the City of Edinburgh. One of these was 'the yearly payment of ten bolls one firlot three pecks one lippy half wheat half barley'. Although the Laird had bought this house he continued to enter as rent the sum of one hundreds pounds annually. In 1761 he entered twenty-five pounds as the rent of the house in Niddry's Wynd, presumably for part of the year, and seventy-five pounds for a half year's rent for Bristow House; thereafter Bristow House was entered as one hundred pounds.

It may seem extravagant for the Laird to have a town house when he lived so near the City, but it must be remembered that horses were the sole means of transport, and a night journey home after a ball or other entertainment would have taken at least an hour. The town house was no doubt used for entertaining as well.

Charge & Discharge of Cattle bought & sold from Wy. 1759 is an entry which covers a period of a year and a half from July 1759 to

February 1761. It is the only entry of its kind, and the only indication that the Laird went in for farming. Why he did so we do not know, but whatever his reasons he made a fair success of his enterprise. He had a good margin between his buying and selling price and most important of all he chose good stock, for there are no deaths or losses during the period he carried them. He was carrying out his father's ideas of over-wintering animals to bring them to a greater size and more profit which could only be done on the newly enclosed farms.

Any attempt to relate eighteenth-century prices with those prevailing today is an extremely difficult if not impossible task. The social and economic circumstances are so far apart. In the eighteenth century the great majority of Scots worked on the land and many worked very close not to the poverty level but to starvation. The disastrous years at the end of the previous century when whole communities were decimated by starvation and the living scarcely had the strength to bury the dead, were still remembered as 'King William's Ill Years'. Farm enclosures, new methods and new crops had improved things so that the famine year of 1758 did not take such a frightful toll; but it was still a fact that a good place in one of the big houses gave a better living than the struggle on the land. It is not to be wondered at if the peasant's brothers and sons took service for a low wage where good clothes, a warm bed and ample food rewarded work, which compared with that on the farm was light. Furthermore there was a little money in his pocket on term day, and perhaps most important there was the companionship of his fellows and opportunity for promotion.

SUMMARY OF EXPENDITURE
1758 TO 1763

	1758	1759	1760	1761	1762	1763	TOTAL	%
To My Wife	£ 400 15.6%	£ 740.26.7%	£ 460 18.1%	£ 663 30.5%	£ 573 19.0%	£ 500 26.4%	£ 3336	22.4
My Pocket	490 19.1%	500 17.9	364 14.3	149 6.9	167 5.8	175 9.2	1845	12.4
Our Cloaths	64 2.5	32 1.1	66 2.6	73 3.3	111 3.9	70 3.6	416	2.8
My Stables	277 10.8	329 11.6	406 15.9	248 11.4	478 16.7	372 19.5	2110	14.2
Labouring & Miscellanys	154 6.0	125 4.5	168 6.6	183 8.4	210 7.3	340 17.9	1180	7.9
Servts Wadges & Livery	101 3.9	93 3.3	119 4.7	109 4.9	121 4.2	128 6.7	671	4.5
Plate Meal Malt Wine Etc.	128 5.0	204 7.3	197 7.7	99 4.6	283 9.8	217 11.4	1128	7.6
My Children	905 35.2	716 25.8	718 28.2	586 26.9	829 30.0	— —	3754	25.3
My House in Edin[r].	50 1.9	50 1.8	50 1.9	75 3.4	100 3.3	100 5.2	425	2.9
TOTALS	2569 100	2789 100	2548 100	2185 100	2872 100	1902 100	14,865	100

Note: In the above summary the Laird's mistakes in addition have been corrected.

SUMMARY OF EXPENDITURE

1728 TO 1763

	To My Wife	To My Pocket	To Our Cloaths	To My Stables	To Labour & Miscellanys	To Servts Wadges & Livery	To Plate Meal Malt & Wine	To My Children	To My House In Edinr	Totals
1728–33	2839 36.2%	1134 14.5%	605 7.7%	1060 13.5%	1275 16.2%	303 3.8%	637 8.1%			7,853
1734–39	2678 31.0%	1044 12.0%	539 6.2%	886 10.2%	1439 16.7%	421 4.8%	1213 14.0%	360 4.1%	75 1.0%	8,655
1740–45	3084 24.5%	1770 14.0%	648 5.1%	1447 11.4%	1247 9.9%	623 4.9%	1012 8.0%	2470 19.6%	325 2.6%	12,626
1746–51	2034 13.7%	2069 13.9%	417 2.8%	1287 8.7%	1361 9.2%	691 4.6%	1043 7.0%	5638 38.1%	295 2.0%	14,835
1752–57	2917 20.8%	1261 9.0%	298 2.1%	1665 11.8%	1255 9.0%	526 3.7%	899 6.4%	4930 35.1%	300 2.1%	14,051
1758–63	3336 22.5%	1845 12.4%	416 2.8%	2110 14.2%	1180 7.9%	671 4.5%	1128 7.6%	3754 25.3%	425 2.8%	14,865
	16,888 23.3%	9123 12.5%	2923 4.0%	8455 11.6%	7757 10.6%	3235 4.4%	5932 8.1%	17,152 23.6%	1420 1.9%	72,885

THE CASH BOOK

Discharge for the years 1721, 1722, 1723, & 1724 stated in my old book extends to			£1721 6 8
Discharge for the year 1725 extends to			£353 12 4
Discharge for the years 1726 & 1727 extends to			£1868 14 9
Discharge for the year 1728			
1728	To My Wife	£581 10 6	
	To My Pocket	£126 15 6	
	To Our Cloths	£191 14 6	
	To Stables	£172 6 8	
	To Labouring & Missilanys	£203 9 4	
	To Meal Malt & Wine	£107 7 7	
	To Servts Cloths & Wadges	£61 1 4	£1444 5 5
1729	To My Wife	£508 3 6	
	To My Pocket	£189 12 4	
	To My Cloaths	£20 10 8	
	To Stables	£312 17 9	
	To Labouring & Missilanys	£169 16 0	
	To Meal Malt & Wine	£90 7 6	
	To Servts Cloaths & Wadges	£39 6 11	£1330 14 8
1730	To My Wife	£373 6 4	
	To My Pocket	£383 19 0	
	To Our Cloaths	£126 5 0	
	To My Stables	£213 17 9$\frac{2}{3}$	
	To Servts Wadges & Cloaths	£46 2 0	
	To Labouring & Missys	£87 8 3	
	To Plate meal Wine &c	£111 17 9$\frac{1}{3}$	£1342 16 2
1731	To my Wife	£500 0 0	
	To my Pocket	£146 11 0	
	To Our Cloaths	£71 11 6	
	To My Stables	£177 2 7	
	To Servts Wadges & Cloaths	£32 5 0	
	To Labouring & Missys	£121 6 10	
	To Plate Malt Wine &c	£76 7 10	£1125 6(1) 9

Year	Item	Amount	Total
1732	To My Wife	£447 0 0	
	To My Pocket	£157 8 6	
	To Our Cloaths	£142 15 9	
	To my Stables	£83 7 8	
	To Servts Cloaths & Wadges	£52 12 6	
	To Labouring & Missys	£356 17 1	
	To Plate Malt & Wine	£174 6 2	£1414 7 8
1733	To my Wife	£400 0 0	
	To my Pocket	£129 17 7	
	To our Cloaths	£52 8 6	
	To my Stables	£101 5 0	
	To Servts Cloaths & Wadges	£71 16 6	
	To Labouring & Missys	£337 9 10	
	To Plate Meal Malt & Wine	£78 6 10	1171 4 3
1734	To My Wife	£413 2 6	
	To My Pocket	£120 12 3	
	To our Cloaths	£10 5 0	
	To my Stables	£183 6 8	
	To Servts Cloaths & Wadges	£57 14 10	
	To Labouring & Missys	£340 12 10	
	To Plate Meal Wine &c	£223 8 0	1349 2 1
1735	To my Wife	£430 5 9	
	To my Pocket	£151 15 8	
	To my Cloaths	£236 3 0	
	To my Stables	£204 5 11	
	To Servts Cloaths & Wadges	£66 16 0	
	To Labouring & Missys	£209 12 11	
	To Plate malt Wine &c	£119 3 7	1418 2 10
1736	To my Wife	£500 0 0	
	To my Pocket	£158 10 6	
	To our Cloaths	£36 5 3	
	To my Stables	£106 10 7	
	To Servts Cloaths & Wadges	£88 8 0	
	Labouring & Missys	£211 5 9	
	To Plate Malt Wine &c	£119 3 7	1189 9 1(2)

Year	Item	Amount	Total
1737	To my sons at Dalkeith	£52 0 0	
	To my wife	£435 0 0	
	To my pocket	£151 19 3	
	To our Cloaths	£22 18 0	
	To my Stables	£195 0 4	
	To Servts Cloaths & Wadges	£73 2 8	
	To Labouring & Missys	£210 13 0	
	To Plate Malt Wine Jewels	£462 12 11	1603 6 2
1738	To my Wife	£400 0 0	
	To my Pocket	£206 8 3	
	To our cloaths	£10 8 5	
	To my Stables	£65 5 3	
	To Servts Cloaths & Wadges	£64 19 4	
	To Labouring Building & Missys	£200 7 10	
	To Plate Meal Wine Malt	£168 7 6	
	To my sons at Dalkeith	£134 19 10	
	To the Rent my house in Edinr for half a year from Wy 1738	£25 0 0	1275 16 6[3]
1739	To my Wife	£500 0 0	
	To my Pocket	£255 2 3	
	To our Cloaths	£224 2 10	
	To my Stables	£132 18 11	
	To Servts Cloaths & Wadges	£70 1 1	
	To Labouring & Building &c	£265 14 8	
	To Plate Wine Meal Malt	£151 17 0	
	To my sons at School	£172 6 0	
	To a years rent of my house	£50 0 0	1822 2 9
1740	To my Wife	£500 0 0	
	To my Pocket	£232 1 2	
	To our Cloaths	£20 0 4	
	To my Stables	£116 13 10	
	To Servts Cloaths & Wadges	£68 13 3	

Year	Item	Amount	Total
1740	To Labouring Missys &c	£246 0 3	
	To Plate malt Jewels Wine	£267 17 9	
	To my sons at Dalkeith	£201 9 3	
	To a years rent of my house	£50 0 0	1702 15 10
1741	To my Wife	£500 0 0	
	To my Pocket	£192 3 9	
	To our Cloaths	£161 6 0	
	To my Stables	£211 0 6	
	To Servts Cloath & Wadges	£64 5 8	
	To Labouring & Building	£229 4 3	
	To Plate Wine Meal	£126 9 1	
	To my sons at School	£238 10 10	
	To a years rent of my house	£50 0 0	1773 0 1
1742	To my Wife	£500 0 0	
	To My Pocket	£295 9 6	
	To our Cloaths	£129 19 3	
	To my Stables	£272 17 5	
	To my Servts Cloaths & Wadges	£66 5 6	
	To Labouring & Missys	£232 14 10	
	To Plate Wine Malt	£148 12 4	
	To my children	£489 18 10	
	To my house rent in Edr	£50 0 0	2185 17 8
1743	To my Wife	£400 0 0	
	To my Pocket	£138 7 10	
	To our Cloaths	£23 6 6	
	To my Stables	£319 4 9	
	To my Servts Livery & Wadges	£68 17 6	
	To Labouring Missys &c	£228 5 8	
	To Plate Wine meal Malt	£223 19 10	
	To my Children	£418 15 9	
	To a years Rent of my house in Edr	£50 0 0	1870 17 10

Year	Item	£	s	d	Total
1744	To my Wife	£628	0	0	
	To my Pocket	£462	6	4	
	To our Cloaths	£212	0	8	
	To my Stables	£328	2	3	
	To my Servts Wadges & Liveries	£92	7	0	
	Labouring & Missys	£335	5	9	
	To Plate Wine Meal Malt	£100	14	3	
	To my Children	£557	8	4	
	To my house rent in Edinr	£50	0	0	2766 4 7
1745 & 1746	To my Wife	£1112	4	3	
	To my Pocket	£901	6	9	
	To our Cloaths	£204	2	4	
	To my Stables	£398	12	0	
	To my Servts Wadges & Livery	£152	0	1	
	To Labouring & Missys	£527	5	10	
	To Plate Wine Meal Malt	£288	10	1	
	To my Children	£1129	13	6	
	To my house rent in Edr	£150	0	0	4863 14 10
1747	To my Wife	£510	0	0	
	To my Pocket	£540	15	0	
	To our Cloaths	£14	16	6	
	To my Servts Wadges & Cloaths	£76	18	0	
	To Labouring Building &c	£186	2	2	
	To plate Wine Meal Malt	£155	10	10	
	To my Children	£854	0	3	
	To my house rent in Edinr	£50	0	0	
	To my Stables	£138	3	2	2526 6 11
1748 & 1749	To my Wife	£968	18	0	
	To my Pocket	£464	12	8	
	To our Cloaths	£60	16	16(4)	
	To my Stables	£424	14	10	
	To Servts Liveries & Wadges	£161	0	1	
	To Labouring & Missys	£452	16	11	
	To plate meal Wine Malt	£277	8	4	
	To my children	£1791	7	2	
	To my house rent in Edr	£70	0	0	4671 15 4

Year	Item	Amount			Total		
1750	To My Wife	£500	0	0			
	To My Pocket	£366	15	2			
	To our Cloaths	£149	18	0			
	To my Stables	£208	6	8			
	To Servts Wadges & Liverys	£90	13	4			
	To Labouring & Missys	£347	15	6			
	To Plate Wine Meal Malt	£223	15	10			
	To my Children	£859	14	3			
	To my house rent in Edr	50	0	0	2796	18	9
1751	To My Wife	£400	0	0			
	To my Pocket	£247	0	9			
	To Our Cloaths	£90	7	6			
	To my Stables	£318	10	0			
	To Servts Liverys & Wadges	£96	18	11			
	To Labouring & Missys	£298	12	2			
	To Plate Meal Malt Wine	£241	14	8			
	To my Children	£1577	0	3			
	To my house rent in Edr	£50	0	0	3320	4	3
1752	To my Wife	£687	10	0			
	To my Pocket	£215	17	10			
	To our Cloaths	£37	3	7			
	To my Stables	£227	15	9			
	To Servts Wadges & Liverys	£80	8	4			
	To Building & Labouring &c	£301	14	4			
	To Plate Meal Malt Wine	£97	9	11			
	To my Children	£736	12	11			
	To my house rent in Edr	£50	0	0	2428	12	8
1753	To my Wife	£450	0	0			
	To my Pocket	£322	9	5			
	To our Cloaths	£38	3	7			
	To my Stables	£177	6	3			
	To Servts Wadges & Liverys	£84	16	6			
	To Labouring Building &c	£173	19	8			
	To Plate Meal Malt Wine	£117	1	2			
	To my children	£1057	17	2			
	To my house rent in Edr	£50	0	0	2471	13	9

Year	Item	£	s	d	Total
1754	To my Wife	£425	0	0	
	To My Pocket	£136	12	11	
	To our Cloaths	£32	15	7	
	To my Stables	£147	17	1	
	To Servts Wadges Livery &c	£93	0	0	
	To Building Missys & Labouring	£195	1	0	
	To Plate Wine Meal Malt	£148	11	2	
	To my children	£697	3	0	
	To my House rent in Edr	£50	0	0	1925 19 9[5]
1755	To my Wife	£450	0	0	
	To my Pocket	106	14	6	
	To our Cloaths	60	12	0	
	To my Stables	323	11	1	
	To Servts Wadges Liverys &c	82	11	2	
	To Building & Missys & Labouring	146	17	7	
	To Plate wine meal malt	108	19	7	
	To my Children	946	16	1	
	To my house rent in Edr	50	0	0	£2276 2 0
1756	To my Wife	£454	12	0	
	To my Pocket	169	11	10	
	To my Cloaths	81	6	7	
	To my Stables	277	6	8	
	To Servts Wadges & Liverys	92	1	2	
	To Building Ditching & Missys	196	10	2	
	To plate wine rum meal malt	328	2	11	
	To my Children	911	3	0	
	To my house rent in Edinr	50	0	0	£2560 14 2
1757	To my Wife	£449	17	8	
	To my pocket	311	6	9	
	To my Cloaths	47	16	7	
	To my Stables	512	7	5	
	To Servts Wadges & Livery	94	10	8	
	To Ditching Building & Missys	241	2	7	

1757	To Plate Wine Meal Malt	100 16 4	
	To my Children	585 15 3	
	To my house rent in Edinr	50 0 0	£2393 13 3
1758	Discharged		
Feb 22	To my wife for our family	£50 0 0	
June 9	To my Wife for our family	150 0 0	
Novr	To my Wife for our family	200 0 0	
	400		
	To my pocket	489 18 3	
	To my Cloaths	64 10 2	
	To my Stables	277 1 1	
	To my Servts Wadges & Liverys	101 7 11½	
	To building & Misselanys &c	153 13 10	
	To Plate Wine Meal Malt	128 3 9	
	To my Children	905 3 5	
	To my House rent in Edinr	50 0 0	
	Total 1758	£2569 19 6	
1759	To my Wife when in London with me	£290 0 0	
Js Stodert			
	Pd my Wife's journey to London by £50 taken from the Bank and now repayd	50 0 0	
May	Pd my Wife towards our family	200 0 0	
Novr	Pd my Wife for our family	200 0 0	
	740		(should read
	To my pocket	217 6 8	£499 14 11½)
	To my Cloaths	32 0 0	
	To my Stables	324 2 1	(329 2 1)
	To my Servts Wadges & Liverys	93 4 4	
	To Building Misselanys &c	125 4 3	
	To Plate Wine Meal Malt	204 9 8	
	To my children	715 12 4	
	To my house rent in Edinr	50 0 0	
	Tottal 1759	2501 19 4	(2788–1–7½)

		£	s	d	
1760	Pd my Wife for our family	50	0	0	
	Pd my Wife for our family	200	0	0	
	Pd my Wife for our family	210	0	0	
	460				
	To my Pocket	264	8	6	(364–8–8½)
	To my Cloaths	66	1	0	
	To my Stables	405	13	10	
	To my Servants Livery & Wadges	119	4	2	
	To building misselanys &c	168	11	4	
	To plate wine meal malt	97	6	5	
	To my children	717	19	6	
	To my house rent in Edin[r]	50	0	0	
	Tottal 1760	2349	4	9	(2449–4–11½)

		£	s	d
1761	Discharge			
March 17	To my Wife for our family	50	0	0
May 13	Pd my Wife to buy furniture for Ross House	58	0	0
June 1	Pd my wife for our family	250	0	0
Nov[r] 25	Pd my wife for our family	250	0	0
	Pd my wife to buy furniture for Bristow house	55	5	0
	663–5			
	To my pocket	148	13	0
	To my cloaths	72	16	0
	To my Stables	248	11	10
	To my Serv[ts] Wadges & Liverys	109	0	7
	To building Misselanys Gardiners &c	183	(13	10)[(6)]
	To Plate Wine Meal Malt	98	17	9
	To my children	586	6	8
	To my house rent in Niddrys Wind to Wy 1761 £25			
	To half a years Rent of Bristow house to Mts 1761 £50	75	0	0
	Tottal 1761	£2186	4	8

1762	To my Wife to buy furniture for Bristow house	3	0	0	
June 3	Pd my Wife for my family from Wy to Marts 1762	250	0	0	
	Pd my Wife to buy furniture for Bristow house	70	0	0	
Sepr 11	Pd my Wife for our family (by a cash draught)	30	0	0	
Novr 27	Pd my Wife for our family	220	0	0	
	573				
	To my Pocket	166	0	8	(167 0 8)
	To my Cloaths	112	16	6	
	To my Stables	477	18	0	
	To my Servants Wadges & Liverys	120	16	4	
	To misselanys Gardings Building &c	209	16	0	
	To Wine Meal Malt plate	283	9	5	
	To my Children untill provided by marriage Contracts & then only to my son James	828	15	0	
	To a years rent of Bristow house & park to Mts 1762 possest by my family	100	0	0	
	1762 Tottall	£2872	11	11	(2873)
1763	Discharge				
Feby 4	To my Wife for our family	50	0	0	
March 3	To my Wife for our family	30	0	0	
May	To my Wife for our family	170	0	0	
	To my Wife for our family	50	0	0	
Augt	To my Wife for our family	200	0	0	
	500				
	To my Pocket pr accts	175	2	3	
	To my Cloaths pr accts	70	8	1	
	To my Stables pr accts	360	13	9	(312 13 9)
	To my Servants Wadges & Liverys	128	11	5	

Augt	To Building Ditching Gardens Misselanys &c &c	340	4	3				
	To Wine Meal Malt Rum &c	127	8	3		(217	8	3)
	To a years rent of Bristow house possest by my family & for the rent of the little park to My 1763	100	0	0				
	1763 Tottal	£1799	8	0[7]		(1904	8	0)
26	To my Wife for our family	30	0	0				
Feby	To my Wife for our family	20	0	0				
	Given my Wife in a present	20	0	0				
June 4[8]	Pd my Wife for our family	200	0	0				

Note

(1) The Laird made a mistake in his addition; the correct sum should be eight shillings.
(2) The correct sum here is nine shillings and no pence.
(3) The correct sum here is sixteen shillings and five pence.
(4) Although the Laird wrote 16 pence he added it up correctly as one shilling and four pence.
(5) The correct total for 1754 is £1926. 0. 9.
(6) This is the first mention of 'Gardiners'. This entry is partly obliterated but the sum in brackets gives the correct total and is a possible reading.
(7) The correct total for 1763 should read £1802. 8. 0.
(8) The Laird died on October 13th 1764; he kept his accounts to within four months of his death.

Discharge of Pocket Mony 1758

Jay[r] 13	Pd[1] Doctor Clerk a consultation about my Wife's health	2	2	0
	Pd for a Fox painting &c at a roup[2] in the abbey	5	10	0
	Pd Mr. Murray[3] my beat lost at Kelso by Lord Aboyne turning without a post	42	0	0
26	Pd Mr. Rattray[4] a consultation about my wifes health	2	2	0

Date	Item	£	s	d
Feby 8	Given Miss Sinclair[5] in a present	3	2	0
	Given in Charity to the poors (hospital) maintenance	1	1	0
	Pd my proportion of our expences by delaying the Hunters Ball[6]		15	6
	Pd Mr Smith for tuneing the harpiscord[7] to July 1757	2	2	0
18	Pd the Chairman[8] for 5 weeks attendance	5	5	0
20	Spent in Drinkmony[9] at Tinninghame Chaise hire &c	1	11	6
22	Pd for 2 sticks of Black wax paper & triffles		6	0
March 6	Pd the Chairmen for another weeks attendance	1	1	0
13	Pd my livery servts[10] for upsets board wadges letters Crows 3 sheep stoping fox earths Tobacco, mending Tubs &c &c	4	13	4
16	Spent for my horses at Edinr & Drinkmony at Calder	1	3	6
	Pd for a new cover to my hunting whip		5	0
31	Pd Dr. Clerk more for attending my Wife	2	2	0
	Pd Mr. Rattray for blooding & attending my Wife	1	1	0
April 5	Spent in my pocket, with the Hunters, for tickets to play-house, Chairhire, Assemblys, coffee house loss on Hercules[11] at Leith & all other expenses throw the winter to the date	78	0	0
	Pd Mr MackPherson for teatching Clema on the harpsicord	1	11	6
	Given my nurse in Charity		10	0
20	Paid my Livery Servts all board Wadges upsets & accts for pouder[12] Oyle Dead horses Tobacco, Turnpikes &c due to ye date	2	18	7
May 12	Pd Mr. Baillie for Lord Mansfields print		3	0
	Given my Wife in a present	1	1	0
	Pd for Mary Kelly[13] & Thos Jackson in Charity		18	4
	Pd Willie Jack for a Lock & bands		1	8
	Pd Dr Gibson[14] for blooding my Wife a blister &c	1	1	0
	Pd George Stodert[15] for assisiting me during his fathers illness		10	6

1758. Discharge of Pocket mony 1758

Jany 13	Pd Doctor Clerk a consultation about my Wifes health	2 2
	Pd for a Fox painting &c at a roup in the abey	5 10
	Pd Mr Murray my bett lost at Kelso by Lord Aboyn turning within a post	42
26	Pd Mr Rattray a consultation about my Wifes health	2 2
Feby 8	Given Miss Sinclair in a present	3 2
	Given in Charity to the poors (hospital) maintenance	1 1
	Pd my proportion of our Expences by delaying the Hunters ball	15 6
	Pd Mr Smith for tuneing the harpsicord to July 1757	2 2
18	Pd the Chairmen for 5 Weeks attendance	5 5
20	Spent in Drinkmony at Tinninghame Chaise hire &c	1 11 6
22	Pd for 2 Sticks of Black Wax paper & trifles	6
March 6	Pd the Chairmen for ane other Weeks attendance	1 1
13	Pd my Livery Servts for Upsets turnpikes boardwages letters Crows 3 sheep sloping for Earths, Tobacco, mending Tubs &c &c	4 13 4
16	Spent for my horses at Edinr & Drink mony at Calder	1 3 6
	Pd for a new Cover to my hunting Whip	5
31	Pd Dr Clerk more for attending my Wife	2 2
	Pd Mr Rattray for blooding & attending my Wife	1 1
April 5	Spent in my pocket, with the hunters, for Tickets to play-house, Chairhire, Assemblys, Coffee houses, Loss on Hercules at Leith & all my other Expences throw the winter to the date	78
	Pd Mr Mackpherson for teatching Clemna on the harpsicord	1 11 6
	Given my Nurses in Charity	10
20	Pd my Livery Servts all boardwadges Upsets vacto for pouder Oyle Dead horses Tobacco, Turnpikes &c due to this day date	2 18 7
May 12	Pd Mr Bailie for Lordy Mansfields print	3
	Given my Wife in a present	1 1
	Pd for Mary Kelly & Thos Jackson in Charity	18 4
	Pd Wille Jack for a Lock & bands	1 8
	Pd Doctor Gibson for blooding my Wife a blister &c	1 1
	Pd George Stodert for assisting me during his fathers illness	10 6
	Pd for Castairs School repairs & to the poor	15 9
	Pd maintenance to Liberton poor to Lambas 1758	1 18 7
	Pd maintenance to Carnwath poor to Marts 1758	3 16 7
June 13	Pd for Drugs to cure 5 people bit by a mad Dog in 1757 at Giving Mill	3 3
	Pd for 12 bottles of Wine when elected President of the Archers	1 4
21	Pd my Livery Servants all Turnpikes Upsets boardwadges Oyl kill Crows or any other thing due to the date	2 11 7
	Pd George Neilson for all Bows to Charle arrows &c	10 6
Sepr 14	Pd for 2 new Seals & a new Gold Watch Chaine	5
	Pd for the Carriage of a box from Scotland	1 5 2
		183 3 7

Facsimile of a page from the Cash Book.

Date	Item	£	s	d
May 12	Pd for Carstairs[16] school repairs & to the poor		15	9
	Pd for maintenance to Liberton poor to Lambas 1758	1	18	7
	Pd for maintenance to Carnwath poor to Marts 1758	3	16	7
June 13	Pd for Drugs to cure 5 people bit by a mad Dog in 1757 at Goring Mill[17]	3	3	0
	Pd for 12 bottles of Wine when elected President of the Archers	1	4	0
21	Pd my Livery Servants all Turnpikes Upsets board Wadges oyl Kill'd Crows or any other thing to the date	2	11	7
	Pd George Neilson for all Bows to Charle[18] arrows &c		10	6
Sepr 14	Pd for 2 new Seals & a new Gold Watch Chaine	5	0	0
	Pd for the Cariage of a box from Scotland	1	5	2
	Given in Charity to Mr. Alvis & others		15	6
	Pd for Ferguson's book of Astronomy		18	0
	Given in Drinkmony to George Borthwick[19]		10	6
	Spent in my journey to [20] Cambridge London Harwich for a Licence & passage, at Rotterdam Helvoet Sluise at London, house rent Washing Servts Coach drinkmony from London to Dryden posting &c &c	165	6	10
	Pd Wm Kelly his expences in returning from Cambridge with my Chaise & horses & when resting at Huntingdon	6	11	10
	Given at Lady Stairs desire to Mrs Browns lottery	1	0	0
	To my coaliers on my Birth day[21]		10	6
	To my nurse		5	0
	Pd my livery Servts board Wadges upsets &c	2	5	7
	Pd ane old debt for triffles to Mssrs Livinstone & Sympson	1	9	0
	Pd[22] Jack Smith his Acct when he left me		2	2
	Pd the Charges of 2 terriers sent by me to Archdeacon Cuninghame		5	0

			£	s	d
Oct	5	Pd Wm Kellys board wadges at Carnwath & for his sons work	1	0	0
		Spent for Lodgings & Eating at Kelso Hunters meeting £5=4			
	21	Pd for my horses grooms, beagles warm water &c besides the [23] 6 bolls of meal laid in by the Council in Full for all £15=10	19	14	0
		Spent in Drinkmony at Mr. John Pringles		12	6
	24	Pd my grooms & Livery Servts for upsets board wadges turnpikes for a whip for harnas Oyle pouder soap hoove salve & every demand any of them has of this date	3	18	7
	26	[24]Spent for triffles ere I set out from Dryden to London	2	10	0
	30	Spent in my journey from Dryden to Morpeth £1=10			
		Given my coachman to carry his expences & horses Home £1=1	17	1	0
Novr		Spent from Morpeth to London £14=10			
		Pd for a chariot hired charges &c to Jayr 1759	21	6	0
		[25]Pd Wm Mackyes accts for eating washing &c to Do	17	9	3
Decr		Pd Mr Tervits (?) Servts in Drinkmony to do	3	3	0
		Pd Mrs Balder for goods sent by her to my newphew at Dryden	2	0	0
My Wife Novr & Decr		Pd Wm Anderson as gamekeeper to Marts 1758		13	0
		Pd the maintenance of Carnwath poor to Wy 1758	3	16	7
		Pd the maintenance of the Liberton poor to Do 1759	1	18	9
		Pd for my tennents Dinners when they pay'd their rents at Carnwath	1	17	0
		Pd Mr James Scott for 2 Gowns to my Daughters			
		Pd James Stodert his expences to the date	2	7	8
		Pd Dr Clerk for attending Phemie[26]	2	2	0
		Pd Mr Smith for tuning the Harpsicord & Spinet to June 1758	1	1	0

		£	s	d
	Pd for Expresses to Kelso with my letters weeding some corns &c		17	4
	Given my Wife		5	0
	Pd for turnpikes & cleaning Carnth Clock & a chest from Dalkeith		6	7
	Pd for a present to my Wife at Mrs Jacks rouping	1	8	0
	Pd Dryden Gardiners &c for shooting Crows		7	0
Novr	Pd Henderson all pouder & shot to the date	1	2	0
Decr	Pd for upsets & turnpikes to the date		19	1
	Pd Mr Bell to Marts 1758	10	0	0
	Pd for Drinkmony at delivering my hay in Edinburgh		5	7
	Pd for postages to Bailie Mickle to the date & for some triffles		5	4
	Pd for 4 bolls of meal & given Widow Lamb & Borthwick in Charity	3	0	0
	Pd Clerk 8 pecks of meal with my setting Dog		7	6
	Pd for some goods to my Wife sent from London (& stated to me at my Clearance Sepr 1759 with Mr Fairholme) in July 1758	5	1	0
	Sum 1758	489	18	3

Notes

(1) The health of the family is referred to several times, and the primitive state of medicine is illustrated by these references. Fergusia recovered from whatever ailment she suffered at this time, but she only survived her husband by one year.

(2) A roup was, and still is, an auction sale. The Abbey was presumably Holyrood.

(3) Mr. Murray was most likely Murray of Broughton which family was friendly with the Lockharts. Beat is to be read as bet; Lockhart lost the very considerable sum of forty-two pounds because his nephew, Lord Aboyne, went off the course. There are very few mentions of Lockhart losing a bet.

(4) Mr. Rattray may have been the Laird's brother-in-law; his youngest sister, Mary, married a Surgeon of that name.

(5) Miss Sinclair was a cousin of the Lockharts and lived only a mile or so away at Roslin. She was Maid of Honour at the wedding of Clementina, the Laird's eldest daughter.

(6) The Hunters' Ball was given by the Honourable Company of Hunters of which Lockhart was President.

(7) Clementina played the harpsichord.

(8) Chairmen carried ladies and gentlemen through the streets to prevent them dirtying their clothes.

(9) Drinkmony, or as the French would say 'pour-boire'.

(10) The Laird's servants carried out many small commissions for him and these were settled up each month. This feature of domestic life is one of the most interesting found in the accounts; men whose wages were only four or five pounds a year laid out what must have been to them quite large sums of money on their master's behalf. Up-sets were 'accidents' or incidental expenses. Crows were vermin and the men got a bounty for killing them. Sheep were for the hounds, and tubs were used in the garden for growing ornamental trees.

(11) Hercules was the Laird's race-horse.

(12) Pouder was gunpowder for shooting the crows; dead horses were again dog food, discovered by the servants during their travels to different parts of the estate and throughout the district. Orders and instructions to the estate staff as well as messages of a more social nature would be carried by hand.

(13) Mary Kelly may have been related to William Kelly the coachman, perhaps his mother. Evidently the Laird looked after the people on the estate in their old age.

(14) Fergusia was still not well and a new physician was called in.

(15) George Stodert was the son of James Stodert the factor.

(16) Carstairs, Liberton and Carnwath were villages on the estate; the land-owners in the parishes were responsible for the maintenance of the poor.

(17) This is a most curious entry; but it can only be coincidence that the Lee branch of the family possessed the Lee Penny which was renowned as a charm with the property of curing the bite of a mad dog.

(18) Charles Lockhart was the tenth child of George and Fergusia; he was born in 1740. Archery was still a very popular sport, and the Royal Company of Archers was a very active body.

(19) George Borthwick was one of the senior servants on the estate, possibly the gardener.

(20) This entry and the one immediately following it describe how the Laird went on a lightning visit to the Continent, visiting London on the way in order to get a licence to travel and to book a passage. He travelled to Cambridge in his own coach driven by Kelly the coachman and then posted on from there. Kelly returned to Dryden, and his expenses for that journey were about equal to his wages for a year. See also text page 2.
(21) There are still extensive coal mines in the area around Dryden.
(22) Jack Smith was one of the grooms who rode the Laird's race horses.
(23) See note 5 on Discharge of Pocket Money 1759.
(24) This was the Laird's second journey south within a few weeks; he was undismayed by the approaching winter which would mean short days and bad roads.
(25) William MacKye was a footman who accompanied the Laird and ran his household while he was in London.
(26) The Laird's second daughter Euphemia died of 'an Iliack Passion' i.e. a pain caused by constriction of the bowels; (Cassels N.E.D.). The details of her last illness are given in the correspondence of her sister Clementina, 'She suffered those three days the most extreme pain as I would a slight head ach(e)'.

Discharge on My Cloaths 1758

Jay[r] 12	Pd Mr. Scot for 2 fine hats, & 3 pair white silk stockings	6	5	0
24	Pd for 4 bob wigs got last year and just now from Mr. Thomson	4	0	0
	Pd Bailie Brown's Creditors for Cloaths furnished to me and for a new black silk vest & breatches to Charle	13	9	0
March 6	Pd Thomson for 2 pair buck skine Gloves		10	0
June 8	Pd Hercules[(1)] for cloaths to myself & Charle to the date	8	5	0
	Pd Mr Smart for 2 suits of cloaths to my self & Charle	5	8	0
	Pd Mr Sinclair for 2 pair of white silk stockings to myself	1	16	0

Sepr 14	Pd in Holland for black suit of Cloaths	7	7	0
	Pd for one pair black silk stockings & for a new plain hat	2	8	0
	Pd for altering some Cloaths in London to Mr Knox	1	0	0
	Pd for 4 pair mix't silk stockings for my self	2	15	0
30	Pd for a pair of gloves & 2 pair of shooting stockings		5	10
	Pd for dressing & a new lace to ane old hatt		6	8
Ocr 24	Pd for dressing & a new lace to a hatt		7	2
Novr & Decr	Pd for 4 pairs black silk stockings, & 3 pair worsted stockings	3	17	6
	Pd Mr. Knox for my blew cloath with gold buttons & repairs	6	10	0
	Sume 1758	£64	10	2

Note

(1) Hercules is a curious name for a tailor and it is still more curious that it was the name of one of the Laird's race horses.

Discharge on Stables horses Coach &c[1] 1758

Jayr 12	Pd for a little setting dog	1	1	0
	Pd John Paterson for 20 bolls meal laid up at Carnth	15	0	0
	Pd Jack Smith to acct for Hercules at Leith	6	6	0
Feby 18	Pd Dryden Smith all shoe nails & Work for Jany	1	15	5
March 2	Pd Dryden Smith for the month of Feb. & all work	1	0	5
11	Pd Maclean & Brunton for livers to my hounds	2	4	3
	Pd Braidwood for 36 stone weight of cracklings		18	0
April 4	Pd Dryden Smith all work in March to my horses	2	5	10
	Pd Thos Jackson for attending my dogs to the date		18	0
May 30	Pd James Wallace all shoes & working to my horses to the date	2	2	0

Date	Item	£	s	d
June 2	Pd John Paterson for all straw & corn furnished to me at Carn^th to the date	88	1	2
	Pd John Weir & Wm Cochran for their hay crops 1757	41	15	0
	Pd Wm Cochran John Weir & Thos Mitchell for 51B 8p corn & Straw	30	1	2
	Pd George Aitken for 20 bolls Corn & Straw	13	4	10
	Pd Grant the saidler for mending & triffles to the date	2	10	0
	Pd for one boll of oats from Dalkeith(2)		13	8
8	Pd Dryden Smith for all work to the date	2	3	10
	Pd for all candles to my stables to the date	1	4	6
13	Pd Mr Murray for Phisick & all horse Drugs to the date	4	2	10
15	Pd for Brawn to many different people being all due to the date	3	5	6
20	Pd Jack Smith in full for Hercules at Leith & himself drinkmony &c		13	0
Sepr 14	Pd my Coach & Chaise duty to W^y 1759	6	0	0
20	Pd Lanark Saidler for all repairs to the date		5	0
	Pd Dryden Smith for June July & Aug	4	18	2
	Pd for six Bolls of Dog meall	3	11	10
Oc^r 20	Pd Abel Darnly for Girths & stirop leathers	1	1	0
	Pd for a Grey pounie bought at Kelso	5	15	6
Oc^r 24	Pd Dryden Smith to Oc^r 5	1	18	5
	Pd for covering Kate this summer with Dr Haigs horse(3)		11	6
	Pd for light boots to Jack Smith when he rod Hercules		7	0
By my wife	Pd Andrew Smith for horses drugs & attendance		15	5
Nov^r &	Pd Doctor Blair for horse phisick(4)		4	9
Dec^r	Pd George Lockhart for mending harnass &c	1	12	0
	Pd Carnwath Smith for Shoes to the date	2	7	2
	Pd John Aitchison for Brawn to the hunters to the date		10	0
	Pd Mr. Cleland for 2 new servants saddles & pr disged acct	3	1	6
	Pd Mr. Gardiner for horse Drugs & attendance	3	8	6

Nov^r^ & Dec^r^	Pd Dryden Smith all work at Dryden to Jay^r^ 1759	4	1	7
	Pd for a fringe for the Coach hammer Cloath		12	0
	Pd for 32 bolls of Dog meal to Dryden	14	13	4
	Sume 1758	£277	1	1

Notes

(1) The Laird's expenditure on his stables and kennels must have made a big contribution to the income of the rural population of the district, many of whom were his own tenants.

(2) It is rather strange that one who dealt in grain and meal in a fairly big way should have bought a single boll; perhaps even then Dalkeith oats were renowned for their quality.

(3) Considering his interest in horses the Laird did very little breeding that figures in the accounts; he may have had one or more stallions of his own.

(4) Today one would think it unusual for a doctor to treat horses but the eighteenth-century doctor spent much of his time in the saddle or the chaise, and could apply his medical knowledge to his stock.

Discharge on labouring Building Ditching Books & all other Miscellanys 1758

Jay^r^ 24	Pd Mr Gordon for a new acc^t^ book[1]		11	0
	Pd in full for trenching the new Garding Ground	1	9	0
	Pd hired men for transporting nine beech trees to the Garding		12	6
	Pd Mr. Allen for painting in my house at Edr & at Dryden pr Disge	3	17	0
Feby 18	Pd Dryden workmen to the date	2	6	9
	Pd John Lockhart for 1168 feet of firwood sawing	1	12	5
March 2	Pd Mitchell for 2 pair of cart Wheels furnished last year	2	0	0
April 4	Pd Dryden workmen for Feby sneding[2] levelling &c		18	9
	Pd Dryden workmen for work in March sneding &c &c	2	2	5

		£	s	d
May 12	Pd Mrs Jack for a large Bible for myself	1	1	0
	Pd for a ditch round George Montgomery & Hew Smiths Park[3]	3	3	0
	Pd for a small ditch at Shodshill		2	0
June 8	Pd James Monylas for sawing Deals & Couples at Dryden to the date	3	10	0
	Pd James Monylas for building & all repairs to the date	4	0	0
	Pd Thomas Sinclair for Custome, Ropes, Tar paint &c to the date	2	6	6
	Pd Dryden workmen for April & May	2	6	7
	Pd Wm Spence all Wright Work at Carnwath to the date		13	0
	Pd John Wather all Cariages & work to the date	2	14	0
	Pd for all grinding at Milton Mill to the date		5	2
Sepr 14	Pd for a small ditch at Shodshill		5	8
	Pd Dryden workmen for June July & August	5	10	8
	Pd for Custome of carts with hay sold at Edr		12	0
Ocr 24	Pd Dryden workmen to Ocr 22d		15	0
	Pd for six bolls ten pecks of thorn haughs	1	16	2
By my wife	Pd Purdie for upholding Carnwath house roof to Mts 1758		10	0
	Pd Carnwath Massons all building repairs to Do	2	11	10
	Pd for inning the hay and shearing my Wife's crop[4]	1	13	6
	Pd Carnwath Gardiner for planting to Mts 1758	1	16	0
	Pd Carnwath wright for making gates		12	0
	Pd James Paterson for nails ropes &c		19	1
	Pd Carnwath 3 servants their Wadges to Ms 1748(?)[5]	9	0	0
	Pd Thomas Sinclair & 3 other Servants to Marts 1758	14	0	0
	Pd Dryden Gardiner & 3 lads to Marts 1758	9	0	0
	Pd all lime for building at Dryden repairs &c to Do	3	18	5
	Pd Thos Sinclair for ropes Candles Customs &c to do 1758	2	13	6
	Pd Grahame for all work to Do		14	4

Date	Entry	£	s	d
Ocr 24	Pd Jas Monylas all repairs building the Swine Court &c to Do	3	6	2
	Pd Jas Monylas in part of Mountmarle Gate house &c	2	12	6
	Pd Jas Cleland all Smith work done by him at Dryden	1	15	11
	To 58 bolls 8 pecks meal to Dryden Gardiners & work Servts	43	17	6
	To 8 pecks of meal to my Wife's calves		7	6
	Pd for 13 bolls meal to Ormiston & Crawford at Carnwath	9	15	0
	Sume 1758	£153	13	10

Notes

(1) No doubt the actual account book from which this is copied.
(2) Sneding (snedding) the process of removing the branches of a tree after felling.
(3) The ditching that was going on on the estate indicates that agricultural improvements were continuing.
(4) There are several references in the accounts to Fergusia Lockhart's farming operations.
(5) Surely a misprint by the Laird for 1758.

Discharge on Meal, Malt, Ale, Rum plate Wine &c 1758

Date	Entry	£	s	d
Jay 26	Pd for an import warrant for 12 dozen of Claret to my house in Edr.		16	0
April 5	Pd Maghie & Stewart for a part of the Hunters punch	1	4	6
5	Pd Mr Wilson for 2 hogheads of Strong ale	5	6	6
June 8	Pd Baillie Wilson for all rum to the date	15	0	10
	Pd James Stodert for ale & Spirits to my family at Carnwath	10	10	0
	Pd Dd. Hunter for ale to Dryden to the date	13	17	6
17	Pd My lady Stair for curran(1) wine made for us	4	3	7½
	Pd my Plate Tax to July 1759	2	15	0
	Pd Mr Marjoribanks for Wine in London	1	13	0

			£	s	d
My Wife Nov & Dec	Pd for ale to my family at Carnwath to Mts. 1758		7	3	3
	Pd for 8 bolls of meall bought to my family at Dryden		4	5	0
	Pd for fraught (freight) of Rum & Madeira from London and for corks when bottled		1	16	0
	Pd for all Alle to my family at Dryden from Dd Hunter		21	9	2
	Pd for 39 bolls 2 pecks, 2 lippies, meal to my family at Dryden		29	7	2
	Pd for 12 bolls 12 pecks to my family & Servts in Carnwath		8	16	3
		Sume 1758	£128	3	$9\frac{1}{2}$(2)

Notes

(1) Curran—currant(?)

(2) One hundred and twenty-eight pounds seems to be a large sum to spend under this heading but examination of the account reveals that almost half of it went to ale and this would have been the universal drink for all servants and employees, probably being served two or three times a day. There would also be a considerable amount of entertaining which would account for the claret and rum. Meal took up a third of the expenditure.

Discharge on My Servts Wadges Cloaths &c 1758

			£	s	d
June 8	Pd Stenhouse for tyking(1) frocks to my Servts to the date		1	11	6
	Pd Dryden Taylor all work to the date		3	9	6
13	Pd Mr Smart for all Livery Cloaths to the date		9	17	0
Sepr 14	Pd for new buckskine breatches to William	£1:5			
	Pd for a new hat & lace to Do.	£1:			
	Pd for a suit of new Livery Cloaths to Do.	£4:	6	5	0
Novr & Decr in London	Pd for Livery Cloaths to my footman in London		4	0	0
	Pd for two hats to my Coachman & footman			18	0
	Pd my Footman Robertsons Wadges in London to Jayr 1759		3	3	0

		£	s	d
By my wife				
Novr & Decr	Pay'd Carnwath Taylor for repairs to Servts Cloaths &c		9	4
	Pay'd James Stodert, Wm. Grahame, Wm. Kelly, Jas Purdie Thos Borthwick the postilion, John Malcom & Wm Mackye their Wadges to Marts 1758	58	0	0[2]
	Pd Charles Reid to acct of Wadges	1	0	0
	Pd Jack Smith half a years Wadges to Whity 1758	5	0	0
	Pd Wm. Grahame for a years meal Bolls 6 Pecks 8	4	17	6
	Pd for 3 bolls 14 pecks to Kelly Purdie & dogs at Carnth	2	17	1½
	Sume 1758	£101	7	11½

Notes

(1) Tyking: Chambers Scots Dictionary gives 'tyke, n. Tick, ticking; the case of a pillow or bed'. Frocks, perhaps we should say overalls, to protect livery suits when doing dirty work.

(2) This entry gives us a good indication of the wages earned at this date: £58 divided between eight men gives an average pay £7.5.0. (£7.25). Some of the more senior staff such as James Stodart the factor, and William Kelly the coachman, would get more than the average and the grooms and footmen correspondingly less. Jack Smith with five pounds for a half year was well paid; as the jockey who rode the Laird's race horse he would rank above the ordinary grooms.

Discharge on my Children 1758

		£	s	d
Jay 3	Pd Jack Smith in part of my Son's bill to him[1]	21	4	0
	Pd Jack Smith by my own security in full of my Son's bills	92	2	0
26	Given my Daughters in a present	2	0	0
March 10	Pd Miss Keith the value of 10 pistols[2] given by her father to my son Jamie when a prisoner by Mr Keiths letter & her receipts	8	15	0
22	Pd at London to Mr. Fairholme[3] for my Son Jamie's bill on him	50	0	0

March 22	Pd Mr. Fairholme at L my sons bill on him for Cards	100	0	0
	Pd Mr. Fairholme at L all postages to & from my Sons, freight of Essence, Comm^n^, Interest, Exchange of some Cash retain'd at Edin^r^, for Garters & Triffles Ballance at last clearance being all due to him per our stated acc^t^ to this date	19	13	8
31	Given Charle at the Hunters ball	1	1	0
April 8	Given Clementina at the Hunters ball	6	6	0
	Given Phemie at the Hunters ball(4)	5	5	0
June 4	Pd Mr Fairholme at Edin^r^ all interest & Exchange now due to him	1	12	6
	Pd my daughters their allowance from W^y^ to Mart^s^	27	10	0
	Pd Mr. Morton in full for Charle at St. Andrews	10	15	3
Novr 30	Pd my daughters their allowance at Mart^s^ to W^y^ 1759	27	10	0
	Pd James Scott for 2 new Gowns a present to my Daughters	31	10	0
	Pd a Draught of my Son Jamie's to Mr. Fairholme at London	25	0	0
	Pd my Sons bills for Whit^y^ & Lambas & Mart^s^ to Mr. Fairholme London	425	0	0
	Pd my Son Charle bills from June to Mart^s^ to Mr. Fairholme Ed^r^	50	0	0
		£905	4	5

Here ends my family Acct^s^ for the year 1758

Notes

(1) Jack Smith the groom and jockey advanced money to one of the Laird's sons.

(2) James, the second son of the family, was a soldier of fortune, and had first joined the service of the Shah Nadir of Persia; he later joined the army of the Empress Maria Theresa of Austria, and served in it with distinction throughout the War of the Austrian Succession. Eventually he rose to the rank of General and was created a Count of the Holy Roman Empire. There is no record of his having ever been taken prisoner other than this entry in the accounts. The Pistole was a Spanish coin worth about eighteen shillings.

(3) Mr. Fairholme was the Laird's Banker, he had offices both in London and Edinburgh.

(4) The Laird was quite generous to his children when they went to the Hunter's Ball but Charles came off badly compared with his sisters. At this time Charles, the youngest of the family was about eighteen years old.

	Discharge of Pocket Monys 1759			
Jay^{r} 22 London	Pd Mrs Finlayson for house rent from Oc^{r} 30 to the date[(1)]	19	8	6
	Pd Doctor Pringle for attending me when in a feaver	16	16	0
	Pd Mr Forbes for 2^{ce} blooding	1	1	0
	Pd Dr Munro for one visit by mistake	2	2	0
	Pd Mr Bredall for Drugs by a discharged acc^{t}	6	16	6
	Pd Wm Mackye for his care of me in the feaver in a present	1	1	0
	Pd Mr & Mrs Finlayson for their care & attendance upon me in my feaver	10	0	0
	Pd Wm Mackye for washing housekeeping Wine porter &c	9	13	0
	Pd for a pound and half of wax[(2)]		10	6
	Pd for a large fir trunk for cloaths		14	0
	Pd for my chariot post Chaise &c	3	2	0
	Pd in drinkmony at Mr Turles	1	10	0
	Pd for carriage of mure game posted from Edin^{r}		17	0
March	Pd Wm Mackye for asses milk[(3)] Washing stage coach & many triffles	3	0	2
	Pd as a member of St. James Coffee house Club	1	11	6
	Pd Doctor Pringle for attendance & Mr Forbes for bleeding	2	12	6
	Pd Wm Mackye for asses milk washing &c	2	12	6
April	Pd Mr. Bredall for all Drugs &c	4	0	4
	Pd Mssrs Yule & Fairholme all postages to Febry 5 1759 £4 17/- all interest on their acc^{ts} £5 12 2 Comm^{n} at our clearance £5 1 6	15	10	8
	Pd in Drinkmony at Mr Turles	1	10	0

		£	s	d
May	Pd for a picture at a sale at Tuickenhame	3	3	0
	Pd Wm Mackye for asses milk washing newspapers &c	7	0	9
June	Pd for printed linning a present to my Wife	3	1	6
	Pd Wm Mackye for washing & his accts for triffles	3	13	2½
	Pd Mr. Finlayson for ane ennameled Picture of Queen Mary & for setting	5	18	0
	Pd Wm Mackye for a large chest & his accts Washing &c	6	15	9
	Pd for Pick tooth cases for presents & Mr Foot for shipping my trunk	1	5	0
	Pd Mrs Lawson[4] the price of mure game sent to London	3	8	1
	Pd for my chariot & post Chaise in London	72	7	2
Jas. Stodert	Spent in my Journey from London to Dryden, my horses at Morpeth, Drinkmony at Mr. Wharton's at Newcastle & for Riddle[?] Journy. My Wife her maid Myself & Wm. Mackye in all.	40	18	0
Febry	Pd for a box to hold the Hunters books being the value of the meal they laid in at Kelso for my hounds[5]	3	3	0
	Pd my subscription as a hunter for a Year 1759	5	5	0
	Pd for the maintenance of Carnwath poor to Marts 1759	3	16	7
	Pd for the maintenance of Liberton poor to Do.	1	4	1
	Pd for the expences of 2 bucks from Hamilton[6]		18	0
	Pd John Walker all due Carstairs poor for 7 quarters to Augt 1759	1	6	3
	Pd Mr. Bennet for English news papers to April 5th 1759	6	1	1
	Pd for the Scots news papers & advertisements to July 1759 £3–17–7			
	Pd all postages from Decr 1757 to Decr 1758 £7–17–1	10	14	8
July	Pd James Stoderts Expences about my affairs		15	0
	Pd my Nurse in Charity	1	1	0

Date	Item		£	s	d
July	Pd. Expences in Edr. laid out in my absence by Clema.		5	7	5
	Pd. Mary Kelly's house rent in Charity			10	0
	Pd. my Gardiner for his journy & fraught of trees from London		2	2	0
	Pd. for a cow lent to my fowler for his familys support		3	15	0
	Given Thomas Jackson in Charity			12	0
	Pd. the Royal Bank Servts at clearing my Cash acct. with them			5	0
	Pd. Mrs. Lawson for Sugar, Roses, pots &c		2	12	11
	Given Mr. Macdonald in Charity(7)			10	6
Sepr 15	Pd my Livery Servts all Boardwadges & accts to the date		3	19	3
	Spent at Traquaire & Hangingshaw in Drinkmony		2	12	0
	Spent for myself & horses at Windygoull			18	0
Octr 29	Pd. Dr. Clerk for attending my Dr. Phemie	£10			
	Mr. Baillie for Drugs & Attendance	£5			
	Jas Stodert for flannels, Chest & all other expences about my poor Childs funerals(8)	£9–7–5	24	7	5
	Pd by my Dr Phemies request		1	0	0
	Pd. Mrs. Lawson for paper for writing		1	1	0
	Pd. for a dinner to Covn(9) Tennents			5	0
	Pd. for a large carpet to Carnwath dinning room		3	7	6
	Spent in going & returning from Callender			8	0
	Given for blooding my Cattle at Shodshill(10)			1	6
	Pd. for meal in Charity & for triffles			17	6
	Pd. Clerk his sallery as Game keeper to Marts 1759(11)		1	0	0
	Pd. Dunsire herd for keeping my mures			5	0
	Pd. half a years maintenance of Liberton poor to		1	8	11
	Pd. the maintenance of Carnth poor to wy 1760		2	17	6
	Pd for my Tennents dinner at Marts		1	17	0
	Pd for a boll of meal in Charity			8	9
	Pd. Thos Henderson for all Gunpouder to the date		1	0	0

Octr 29	Pd for 8 pecks of meal given in Charity		4	6
	Pd for a dinner at the bridgehouse		15	1
	Pd Jas Frazer for damage done by my cattle to his garden		4	0
	Pd. my Livery Servts all demands for upsets &c Or any other article for hoove salve &c &c in all	4	15	6
	Pd. Mr. Bell to Marts 1759	10	0	0
	Pd. Nicoll for repairs to clocks & watches to Marts 1759	2	18	0
	Pd. for being absent from the Air meeting & my annual payment as a hunter from Marts 1759 to Do 1760	6	6	0
	Pd. ane express to Mr. David Dixon		6	0
	Pd. My postillion to return from Morpeth	1	1	0
Decr	Given at Christmas	1	1	0
	Pd. for Washing boardwadges to Wm. Mackye & Jas Robertson for my own dyet, pouder oyle &c &c	12	17	5
	Pd. for a hat a present to my Daughter £1–1–0 Earrings & necklace to Do £6–9–0	7	10	0
	Pd. Mr. Foot all demands for shipping trunks &c	17	0	0
	Pd. Mrs. Finlayson for Lodgings & fire in London	6	16	6
	Pd. for Coach hire pocket mony, & my journy to & from London	78	5	6
	Pd for a magnifying glass	1	1	0
	Sume 1759	£217	6	8(12)

Notes

(1) The Laird had travelled to London in November 1758, and must have been taken ill soon after his arrival. He was looked after by his personal servant William Mackye and his landlady Mrs. Finlayson.

(2) Wax for sealing letters (?).

(3) Asses milk must have been prescribed by the doctor as a cure for the fever.

(4) Mrs. Lawson is mentioned once or twice as doing a variety of small services; she may have been the housekeeper at Dryden.

(5) The Honourable Company of Hunters had provided meal for the Laird's hounds at the Kelso meeting to the value of £3.3.0. and he bought a box to hold their books for the same amount.
(6) There are several mentions of bucks being brought home from a distance; possibly these were animals killed at meetings of the Hunters and shared out among the members.
(7) It is curious that the formal title of Mr. is given to someone to whom the Laird gave ten shillings and sixpence in charity.
(8) As already mentioned the death of Euphemia is reported in her sister Clementina's letters.
(9) Cov^{n}=Covington a village on the Carnwath Estate. The Laird's brother Alexander took the title of Lord Covington when he was made a judge.
(10) Shodshill is a farm near Carnwath which the Laird had in hand at this time.
(11) The very low rate of pay received by Clerk for his duties as gamekeeper suggests that he was only employed in this capacity part-time, and probably had a croft or small holding to supplement his wages.
(12) The Laird made an error of £282–8–3½ in his addition, the correct answer is £499–14–11½.

Discharge on my Cloaths 1759

Pd. for 2 pair black worsted stockings		12	0
Pd for a black Coat 4 pair Weepers, 4 Cravats, 4 dimity under Waistcoats &c pr Mr Knox acc^{t} disged & also for a suit of plain cloaths	21	4	0
Pd for 2 pair of shoes to Robt Fisher	1	1	0
Pd for a pair of Jocky Boots to Do	1	5	0
Pd for 12 under Stockings for my self	1	13	0
Pd for dressing a new lace to my hat		19	0
Pd for dressing my wigs 13 months in London &c	2	8	0
Pd for dressing ane old hat & a new lace		9	0
Pd Mrs. Lawson for silk handkerchiefs to replace those lost at London	1	7	6
Pd for a pair of black Cloath Breatches (London)	1	1	6
Sume 1759	£32	0	0

Discharge on my Stables Coach Horses Harness &c 1759

		£	s	d
	Pd Wm Kelly for my hunters at London Tuikenhame & returning to Dryden boardwadges &c &c in all	23	4	9
	Pd for my hunter Dunkirk [with Sampsons price]	42	0	0
March	Pd for a black Coach horse	20	10	6
	Pd for a Saddle & Briddle & 4 shoes	1	8	0
	Pd Mr. Grant for Cloaths to Dunkirk &c in London	1	16	0
	Pd my black horse expences in London	7	7	0
Js Stodert	Pd for a boll of beans to my hunters		10	7
	Pd Dryden Smith to June	7	17	7
	Pd my Tennents for 85 bolls of straw at Carnwath	45	7	10
	Pd Dryden Tennts for 79 bolls 12 pks Corn & Fodder	46	10	5
	Pd Wm Cochrane & john Weir for Hay to Dryden Crop 1758	28	15	5
	Pd for bear (beer) to my Daughters mare when ill		5	3
	Pd for straw to my horses at Dryden	9	8	6
	Pd for nolt(1) livers to my hounds at Dryden	2	7	10
	Pd Dryden Smith to the first of July		16	8
	Pd for 16 bolls Dog meal to Carnwath	7	0	0
	Pd my Coach & Chaise Duty to April 1760	6	0	0
	Pd Dryden Smith to the first of Augt(2)	1	18	10
	Pd for a little Sheltie	1	6	8
	Pd Dryden Smith to the first of August	1	10	9
	Pd for a stallion to Kate in June last		11	6
Novr	Pd for 34 bolls Dog meal to my hounds at Carnth	14	2	0
	Pd for old & new straw at Carnwath	3	18	6
	Pd for 14 bolls of oats to my horses at Carnth	5	19	8
	Pd Carnwath Smith pr Disged acct	4	12	4
26	Pd Dr Blair for Phisick & horses Drugs to the date	1	11	6
	Pd for a new Saddle to Wm Cochrane Girths &c to Js Hutton	1	14	0
	Pd Andw Smith for horses Drugs & attendance	1	6	0

Novr 26	Pd Carnwath Couper & Taylor for Stable Work		12	1
	Pd for mending harnass, a pair of boots to my Coachman &c	2	0	0
	Pd Thos Jackson for attending my Dogs		19	6
	Pd Thos Sinclair for 20 bolls Dog meal to my Dogs	8	3	4
	Pd Dryden Smith to Decr 1 1759	4	3	0
	Pd Malcolm Brown all Saddle Work & for a Clog Bag pr Disge	4	3	0
	Pd Grant all Saddle repairs &c pr disged acct to the date	1	14	0
	Pd for a tup(3) a horse brawn from Loanhead	1	1	6
	Pd Dryden Smith for Decr 1759	1	16	0
	Pd for Hay & Straw to the horses [for Clema] in Edinr		18	7
	Pd Wm. Kelly his jouny to Mr Selbys £5–4/- Hunters expences at Mr. Selbys 5–5/- Journy to Dryden 4–4/-	13	13	0
	Sume 1759	£324	2	1(4)

Notes

(1) Nolt—cattle.

(2) There are two entries referring to the Dryden Smith's account for August; perhaps one of them should be dated September.

(3) Tup—ram.

(4) The Laird's addition is in error by £5.0.0., the correct amount should be £329.2.1.

Discharge on my Servants Cloaths & Wadges 1759

	Pd Hired footmen for serving my Wife & me in London in all	10	4	0
	Pd for a new pair breatches & repairs to my footman	2	5	0
Js Stodert	Pd Dryden Taylor to Wy 1759 pr Disged Acct	3	11	0
	Pd for Grey Cloath from Gallashilds for Servts Frocks	1	15	0
	Pd 2 footmen who left my service at Whity 1759	4	0	0

	Pd Charles Reid to acct of his Wadges at M 1759	1	0	0
	Pd my Postillion to acct of his wadges at M 1759	1	0	0
Oct	Pd Alexr Campbell when he left my Service	2	0	0
Nov	Pd John Waddle when he left my service	2	0	0
	Pd Carnwath Taylor to the date		12	8
	Pd Wm. Kelly & other Grooms their livery meals at Carnth	3	14	8
	Pd James Stodert & all my Livery Servts their mony wadges due to them at Marts 1759	56	0	0
	Pd for a hat to Wm Mackye & lace	1	2	0
	Pd for a Suit of Livery Cloaths to Wm McKye (in London)	4	0	0
	In Sume 1759	£93	4	4

Discharge on building Labouring Ditching Books & Miscellanys 1759

	Pd Doctor Campbell for several books when in London	11	5	0
Js Stodert May	Pd Grahame all work at Dryden to June 1 1759	2	19	1
	Pd John Walker for Cariages to Wy 1759		14	0
	Pd for grinding groats at Milton Mill &c to W 1759		5	10
	Pd for Thack(1) for Mountmarle Gatehouse	3	0	0
	Pd James Monylas in full for building Mountmarle Gatehouse	2	12	6
	Pd James Monylas all work at Dryden to Wy 1759	7	15	6
	Pd Thos Sinclairs Acct to Wy 1759	2	0	4
	Pd Grahame all Work at Dryden to the 1 of July		11	8
	Pd for binding 88 Carts of Harlewood(2)	2	4	0
	Pd Hunter & Aikman to acct of their years Wadges at Ms 1759	3	0	0
	Pd for Hay bought at Shodshill by Js Stodert	1	19	4
	Pd for mowing & all Days Wadges at Dryden	2	3	2

	£	s	d
Pd all Workmens Wadges at Dryden for Aug[t]	1	18	8
Pd for mowing ferns[(3)] &c at Dryden	1	0	8
Pd for shearing my Wifes Crop at Dryden	1	15	6
Pd John Lockhart for cutting Logs for firewood	1	7	0
Pd Wm Walker half a years carages to Marts 1759	1	3	6
Pd Carnwath Masons all triffles to the date		17	0
Pd Wm Spence all Wright work to the date		15	0
Pd Ja[s] Paterson for nails candles &c to the date		8	3
Pd for redding[(4)] the drains before Carn[th] house		5	0
Pd Hugh Smith for Wheat Straw to Carnwath Stables	1	5	0
Pd Ormiston & Crawford their Wadges to M[s] 1759	6	0	0
Pd Grahame Ormiston & Crawford a years meal to Do	8	16	3
Pd James Gibson for Drugs to Sick Cows		8	0
Pd James Monylas all work to the date	3	7	0
Pd Tho[s] Sinclair for Ropes tar Custome pr disged acct	2	12	0
Pd for 31 bolls of Lime to Dryden	1	14	0
Pd Tho[s] Sinclair, R[t] Aikman, D Hunter, R Lind & I Kelly all Wadges due to them at Marts 1759	14	0	0
Pd my Gardiner & 3 Lads Wadges to Mart[s] 1759	9	0	0
Pd for 58, B 9p, meal to my Gardiners & work Serv[ts] from Marts 1758 to Do 1759	26	9	0
Pd Dryden Gardiner for thorn haws	1	0	0
Pd for 4 Vollms of Lidia		12	0
Sume 1759	£125	4	3

Notes

(1) Thack—thatch.

(2) Binding—I can only suggest tying in bundles. Harlewood, the wood laths for carrying plaster or harle i.e. rough cast.

(3) Ferns—probably bracken used for bedding.

(4) Redding—cleaning.

Discharge on Ale Malt Rum Wine plate Meal &c 1759

			£	s	d
	Pd Mr Marjoribanks for all wine when in London from him		4	16	6
	Pd Mr. Kirwan for 117 Gallons of Rum	£52–13			
	for 2 Casks of Madaira	£24			
	packing Shipping &c	£1	77	13	0
Js Stodert					
	Pd Rosline Tennents for 50 bolls of barley		26	5	0
	Pd Dd Hunter for malting 50 bolls of barley		6	11	8
	Pd my Plate Duty to 1759		2	15	0
	Pd Dd. Hunter for Ale to Dryden in full pr Disged Acct		3	8	0
My Self	Pd Mr Neilson for fraught(1) of Rum Madaira &c from London		2	6	0
	Pd Mr Birnie for a hogd(2) of Cyder		3	19	0
	Pd for meal to my family when at Carnwath		2	18	4
	Pd all Ale furnished to my family at Carnwath		9	19	0
	Pd Hugh Grahame for 3 bolls of Dunbar malt		2	2	0
	Pd Mr McIntosh for wine furnished me in 1757 & 1758		5	11	0
	Pd for 40 bolls meal to Dryden family		18	1	8
	Pd Mr Kirwan for Malaga Wine		38	3	6
		Sume 1759	£204	9	8

Notes

(1) Fraught—freight.
(2) Hogd—hogshead.

Discharge on my Children 1759

		£	s	d
	Pd for 2 new Gowns sent from London to my Daughters	24	18	0
	Pd Mr Yule & Fairholme in full of my Son Jamies Draughts	25	0	0
	Pd my Daughters their allowance from Wy 1759	27	10	0
	Pd my son Charles Bills from Marts to Wy to Mr. Fairholme Edr.	50	1	6
June 13	Pd my son Charles Bills from Whity to Marts 1759 to Mr Fairholme Edr	55	0	0

Sepr 3	Pd my son Charle in advance for Bills retired (?) from Mr Fairholme Edr	25	0	0
4	Pd Mr Fairholme at Edr all interest on my childrens bills at our clearance	4	7	3
Nov[r]	Sent to Mr Fairholme in London to acct for my Eldest Sons Draughts	300	0	0
	Pd Mr Fairholme [in full for Charle at Marts] at London	25	0	0
	Pd Mr Fairholme at Edr for Exchange for these bills when I payd Mr Fairholme at	3	5	0
	Edr the ball[ce] of all accts & amnt between us being £173 as also £2–7–7 interest on the balances	2	7	7
	Pd my Daughter her allowance from Marts to Wy 1760	20	0	0
	Given Mr Fairholme in London to account for my sons abroad	150	0	0
	Pd for accorns sent by my Sons abroad	3	3	0
	Sume 1759	£715	12	4

Here ends my Accompts for the year 1759

Charge & discharge of Cattle bought & sold from Wy 1759(1)

		BOUGHT	SOLD
	I bought for Shodshill parks 34 cows & a bull at	£68 1 6	
July	I bought 21 wedders for Dryden grass from J[s] Wilson	9 0 0	
Augt.	I bought 10 Highland Cows & sent them to Shodshill	£21 8 0	
Sep[t]	I bought one highland stot(2) and sent it to Shodshill	2 2 0	
Oc[t]	I sold my 34 Cows & my bull from Shodshill		101 16 6
Nov[r]	I bought 20 wedders for Dryden grass from G.M.L.	£8 6 8	
1760 March	I sold my ten highland cows and the highland stot for		31 4 0

		BOUGHT	SOLD
May	I bought 40 Cows for Shodshill at	86 7 6	
Aug^t	I sold my 40 Cows from Shodshill for		124 7 6
Nov^r	I sold my 41 wedders at Prime cost to my Wife		17 6 8
		193 5 8	374 14 8
Decr 1760	I payd for 30 Highland Stots	57 6 5	
Feb 7 1761	I sold 20 of these Stots to John Brunton for		48 0 0
	I sold 4 of these Stots to my Wife for		10 0 0
	I gave 6 of these Stots to my Wife for nothing		15 0 0
		57 6 8	73 0 0

Notes

(1) The Laird made several mistakes in this entry; the total under bought in the first section should read £195.5.8. In the second section the Laird has copied down £57.6.5 as £57.6.8.

(2) Stot—a young cattle beast.

Discharge of pocket mony 1760

Feby 17	Pd to a Collection for supporting the Infirmary	1 1 0
	Pd for a Subscription ball in Edr	1 17 0
21	Pd for Chairmen in Edr	3 3 0
	Spent in taverns playhouse Assembly &c	5 5 0
	Pd for Kees to Mavisbank Wood & 2 Chaoses to Dryden(1)	16 8
	Pd Mr. Douglas in part for Barron de Loudons Geneology advanced by that Genrals order(2)	2 2 0
	Pd Wm Kelly for old Thorns(3) from his Garding	10 6
	Pd for 2 flannel wastcoats a present to Ja^s Stodert	6 0

		£	s	d
March 20	Pd my livery servants for accts triffles upsets &c to the date	7	11	9
	Pd Wm Kelly for going to Hamilton & catching 3 Deers		8	0
	Pd Mr Finlayson for 2 Copys of my Picture set in Gold with Garnet bracelets &c for my With (?wife) & daughter	20	0	0
	Given Clemena in a present	1	1	0
May 24	Spent with Biggar Presbytery about Mr Christes transportation	2	8	0
	Pd Spence for 2 black frames for my Isle		10	0
	Pd the carters for driving three Deer from Hamilton		12	0
	Pd for Carstairs poor to Why 1760		11	3
	Pd for Liberton poor to Do	1	8	11
	Pd for Carnwath poor to Do	2	16	8
	Pd Mary Kelly & others in Charity	1	0	0
31	Pd Wm McKye for eatables before my family came to Carnth	2	16	7
	Pd for a years cleanning Carnth Clock to ye Date		2	6
June 5	Spent at the Bridgehouse		9	8
	Given Andw Smith for helping to buy my Cattle 2 years	1	1	0
	Pd all postages due April 27 at Edinr	5	12	10
	Pd Mr Reid the price of some hay not delivered to him	1	0	10
June 2	Pd my livery Servants all accts for turnpikes &c to ye date	2	14	6
10	Spent at Tinninghame, Yester, Spot, at the review &c for Grass & Servts	2	11	0
	Pd Rosline for fraught & duty of all goods to the date	1	14	1
	Pd for teaching Clema musick last Winter in Edinr	2	2	0
	Pd Mr Smith for tuning the harpsicord to July 1759	1	1	0
August 2	Pd for Wine when I gained the Musselburgh Arrow	1	15	0
	Pd for a pair of Silver knee & shoe buckles a present to my Gardiner		16	6

20	Pd my Servts accts for turnpikes boardwadges upsets &c		3 10 0
	Pd my family expences when Shooting at Carnwath		14 6
27	Pd Mr Fairholmes at London & Edinr		
	interest on their Acct	£18 6 8	
	Do all postages	9 0 5	
	Do for Commn	8 0 9	
	Do for triffles advanced	1 5 6	
27	Pd Mr Fairholme in London the ballance of my former acct when cleared by cash remitted to him all these articles are included in our mutuall discharges of this date	85 15 8	120 9 0
Oct 30	Pd for my hounds at Coupar & their Journys	£4 16 6	
	Hunters at Coupar &c	£14 2 0	
	4 Grooms at Coupar	£4 3 6	23 2 0 [4]
	Pd Wm McKye for board wadges & my small accts	2: 2: 6	
	Spent in my pocket at Coupar, for balls, Collns for Lodging boats &c	21: 5: 6	23 8 0
	Pd for entrymony with Spot for Coupar town Purse	3:18: 0	
	Pd for plating Spot twice at Coupar	10: 6	
	Pd for weights at Do	10: 0	
	Pd Charles my Groom for riding	2: 2: 0	
	Pd for Drinks to my Grooms on Spots Victory	2: 2: 0	13 6 6
	Pd Spot & Charles Expences from their leaving Carnwath untill they returned there	4: 4: 0	
Novr 1	Pd for a Guitar a present to my Wife		6 0 0
	Pd for girths & other triffles to Wm Grahame in full		10 0
	Pd Johnston for bringing home the 2 Bucks from Coupar		10 6

			£	s	d
	5	Pd my expences in my family at Carn[th] before I went for Couper	1	9	5
		Pd for black wax from Mr Gordon & Mrs Lawson		14	0
		Pd for the poor at Carnwath to Wy 1761	2	17	6
		Pd for the Liberton poors Maintenance to Wy 1761	1	4	9
		Pd for my Tennents dinners after paying their Rents	1	17	0
Dec[r]	3	Pd for housekeeping at Carnwath to ye date	3	17	11
		Pd all turnpikes & upsets triffles &c due to my Serv[ts]	5	5	0
		Pd Clerk my Gamekeepr to Wy 1760	1	0	0
		Pd Dunsire herd to Marts 1760		5	0
		Pd Wm Heriot for mending my Pistols		4	6
		Pd James Stodert all his expences in my affairs	2	9	0
		Pd for triffles done to me by Wm Jack & Spence		14	6
		Pd Mr Bell	10	0	0
		Pd for a boll of meal to Wid[w] Liddle in Charity		8	10½
		Given W[m] McKye when he left my service in a present		10	6
	7	Spent in my Journy from Dryden to Eastwell & London	20	17	0
		Spent in house keeping for Coaches Coals Lodgings a footman for board wadges, Drinkmony &c	8	1	6
		Spent in my return to Eastwell at Grantham, fox hunting at Mr Monteiths, Baraby & in returning to Dryden	21	12	0
		Pd for 2 horses sent from this (Goliath & Blott) & Wm Kellys expences with them from Grantham hunting	12	4	1
		Sume 1760	264	8	8½[(5)]

Notes

(1) Kees might be keys and chaoses are perhaps chaises.
(2) Baron de Loudon was one of the Generals in Maria Theresa's army in which the Laird's second son James also held that rank.
(3) The thorns would have been for hedging the newly enclosed fields.

(4) Spot was the Laird's racehorse. This entry gives some indication of the importance of the Race Meeting at Coupar.

(5) The Laird's error here amounts to £100.0.7. The correct amount should be £364–9–3½.

Discharge on my Cloaths 1760

		£	s	d
	Pd Robt Fisher in London for 2 pair of Pumps	1	1	0
May	Pd for a pair of stocking breatches		12	0
June	Pd Hercules for all Cloaths making to ye date	2	13	0
28	Pd Mr Scott for all cloath &c for my Self or family bought of him per his disged Acct of this date	61	0	0
Decr 7	Payd Mr Knox for a short riding coat made in London		15	0
	Sume 1760	£66	1	0

Discharge on Stables, Horses, hounds &c 1760

		£	s	d
Feby 17	Pd for Straw & Hay to 2 horses in Edin^{r}	1	10	0
	Pd Dryden Smith for Jany	1	6	8
March	Pd for 2 bolls of beans for my hunters		14	6
	Pd my coachman for 3 pints nolt feet oyle		5	0
	Pd Purdie for all Livers for the Dogs to ye date	1	2	10
20	Pd for Honny, Brawn, Nitre, Brimstone Candles a briddle, 3 pairs of combs & brushes in full to ye date per my Grooms accts now cleared	5	15	1
	Pd Chrighton for new linning my Coach, for blinds repairs to ye Phaeton & Chaise p^{r} discged Acct	9	10	0
	Pd Malcom Brown for 3 pair Stirop Irons		6	0
	Pd Dryden Smith for Feby & March	2	16	7
	Pd for 2 bolls of Dog meal to Dryden		14	8
April	Pd Grant for repairs &c p^{r} disged Acct		18	0
May 31	Pd John Stodert for all Corn & fodder bought for my horses at Carnth	41	0	0
	Pd Carnwath Shoemaker all harnas & repairs to the date		10	5

Date		£	s	d
May 31	Pd Carnth Taylor for repairs to my horses Cloaths		4	11
	Pd for 24 bolls Dog meal to Carnwath	9	0	0
	Pd Thos Jackson for keeping the Dogs		12	0
	Pd Wm Grahame for Brand, Candles, hoove salve, ropes &c	1	0	0
	Pd for 3 bolls of beans & pease at Carnwath	1	1	0
	Pd for mending my big saddle for 2 Gents Saddles one Clog bag saddle & all repairs to James Hutton	4	12	0
June 5	Pd my coach & Chaise Duty to April 1761	6	0	0
June 9	Pd Wm Kelly Expences in bringing home Spot	3	13	6
	Pd Dryden Smith for April & May	2	18	1
	Pd for 3 threve[1] Wheat Straw for litter to Spot		7	6
	Pd Aitken Cochran Weir & Mitchell for 83 bolls Corn & Straw to Dryden	48	11	3
	Pd Weir & Cochran for their hay Crop 1759	47	6	4
	Pd Loanhead Candlemaker for all Candles Cracklings &c	1	7	3
	Pd for flanell for sweating Cloaths to Spot		11	0
July	Pd Dryden Smith for June	1	16	7
	Pd for six bolls of Dog meal & 2 pecks of Wheat	2	5	9
Augt	Pd for Phisick, Oyle, Brand, Liver brushes & combs &c to Wm Grahame	1	10	0
	Pd for beans to Spot & his & my Grooms expences for 8 weeks at Gilloan for hay, oats, Balls Smith Board-wadges &c	7	9	4
27	Pd a bill I drew upon Mr Fairholme as the price of my horse Spot this article is included in our clearances of this date	105	0	0
Sepr	Pd Dryden Smith for July & August	3	3	8
Novr	Pd Hugh Smith & others for all their Straw for Litter to ye date	5	8	4
	Pd for Bolls of oats from Dr Elder & Govans	2	15	3
	Pd for 24 bolls of Dog meal bought Sepr first 1760	9	12	0
	Pd James Wallace for shoeing my horses to the date	5	17	0
	Pd Thos Jackson 9 weeks keeping my Dogs		13	6

Nov[r]	Pd And[w] Smith all farrier work & Drugs to the date		12	0
Dec[r]	Pd for reins & head stales & bits for six new coach bridles	1	8	0
	Pd for 5 firlots old pease to my hunters		10	0
	Pd for hoove salve to my hunters		10	0
	Pd for washing Spots cloaths & his riders		10	0
	Pd Grant for a new saddle to Spot	1	1	0
	Pd Dryden Smith for Nov[r] & preceedings, for nails, a copper helping, Chimneys &c p[r] disged Acct[(2)]	4	4	10
	Pd Thomas Sinclair for 40 bolls Dog meal to be laid up for my dogs & acct for by him	17	0	0
	Pd Crighton for mending my Coach harnas to the date		9	6
	Pd Sir W[m] Moor for a black Gelding for a hunter	15	15	0
	Pd Mr Crookshanks for a mare for buying & her expences to Grantham 21 / 3 7 6 — By ane order upon Mr Fairholme London	24	7	6
	Sume 1760	£405	13	10

Notes

(1) Threve equalled 24 sheaves.

(2) This entry is unintelligible.

Discharge on my Servants Cloaths Wadges &c 1760

	Pd Wm Mackye to acct of his Wadges at M[s] 1760	2	2	0
	Pd my 2 footmen between them to acct	3	3	0
May 2	Pd my Coachman in part of his Wadges	1	1	0
	Pd James Purdie in part of his Wadges	1	1	0
	Pd W[m] Kelly in part of his Wadges	2	2	0
	Pd for frocks furnished last year to my Coachman & postilion		10	6
	Pd my postilion in part of his Wadges		15	0
	Pd Dryden Taylor to Wy 1760	2	3	10
June 20	Pd Mr Smart all livery cloath furnished to the date	11	5	0

		£	s	d
June 20	Pd for 2 footmens leather caps		6	0
	Pd my footmen in full their Wadges when they left me at Wy	1	9	0
	Pd for 37 yeards Galashields Cloath for Servts frocks &c	2	16	6
	Pd James Purdie more in part of his Wadges	1	0	0
Novr 25	Pd for meal to my Livery Servts & Kate at Carnwath 5 B	2	4	4
	Pd for Breatches from Thomson to my Servts Pr disge	4	2	6
	Pd (besides former payts) James Stodert, Wm Grahame, Wm Kelly, J Purdie W Montgomery, Charles Reid, Thos Borthwick R. Smith Wm Mackye, Donald McDonald, & J Gray in full of all Wadges due to them (& in place of Drinkmony) to Marts 1760	67	7	0
	Pd Mr Caithness for linning pockets, silk threed &c to my Servts Cloaths per along discharged acct	14	0	0
	Pd Wm Mackye for wearing his own frock	1	1	0
	Pd Daniel for wearing his own cloaths (& for them) when he left my service for insolence		14	6
	Sume 1760	119	4	2

Discharge on Misselanys, building books paper Ditching &c 1760

		£	s	d
Feb	Pd Thos Mitchell for a pair of Cart wheels & a brewing pump	1	12	0
March	Pd for a workman with the Gardiners to the date	1	7	0
	Pd for Ditching taking up hedges & planting them round Wm Cochrans park	4	5	10
May	Pd for a new pump, new cart Wheel, six new Chairs & to Wm Spence	2	19	0
	Pd for Hay to cattle up at Shodshill (for winter 1759)	2	2	0
	Pd Purdie for upholding Carnwath Roof to Marts 1759		10	0
	Pd Bennet for a Dunghill		7	6

			£	s	d
June	9	Pd James Monylas all work at Dryden to the date	3	15	0
		Pd Jas Cleland for Iron work to Mountmarle gate &c &c	3	13	6
		Pd for grinding all corn at Dryden to the date		13	0
		Pd my Gardiner for moles kill'd beescapes &c		10	2
		Pd all Days Wadges at Dryden to the date		9	4
		Pd Dryden Timber Acct to Bailie Wilson Pr Disge	13	13	10
		Pd Thomas Sinclair his acct at Dryden to the date	2	15	5
		Pd Peter Gordon for Straw to Dryden Cows & 3 bolls pease	10	8	0
July	2	Pd Dd Hunter & Robt Aikman in part their wadges due Mts next	3	0	0
		Pd for mowing & winning Dryden Hay	2	14	0
		Pd for weeding corns & potatoes		18	8
		Pd for painting Dryden Windows gates &c	3	18	4
		Pd for sawing fir trees into deals for Dryden	4	5	0
Augt		Pd for cutting & sawing trees for tennents houses &c	1	17	0
		Pd for inning Dryden hay Weeding thorn beds & all days Wadges		19	4
		Pd for mowing gathering & inning my fearns	2	13	3
Novr	1	Pd Robt Aikman more in part of his Wadges	1	0	0
		Pd for inning Hay Shearing Dryden Crop & all Days Wadges	2	5	9
	20	Pd James Graham Ormiston & Crawford their meal Wadges to Mts	8	8	0
		Pd Crawford & Ormiston their mony Wadges to Marts 1760	6	0	0
		Pd for meal to Dryden workmen at Carnwath		6	10½
		Pd for some Dung & filling Carts to cover the Coat Croft park	2	18	7½
		Pd Carnwath Massons taylor & Couper		19	1
		Pd James Paterson for nails tar Ropes Greese &c	1	8	11
		Pd Lanark Saidler for Cart Saddles		3	0

		£	s	d
Nov[r] 20	Pd James Monylas all work at Dryden to the date	1	17	0
	Pd Thomas Sinclair for Ropes Customes Tar Candles &c	1	19	9
	Pd James Purdie for upholding Carn[th] Roof to M 1760		10	0
	for plastering my Serv[ts] room at Do		7	6
	Pd Dryden Days Wadges men to the date		16	4
	Pd for bolls of lime to Dryden(1)	2	12	0
Dec[r]	Pd Walker all Cariages due to the date			
	Pd Dryden Glasier for Dryden house to Why 1760	1	10	0
	Stable brew house & Habby new windows		18	10
	Pd my Gardiner & 3 Lads to Marts 1760	9	0	0
	Pd Thos Sinclair, R Lind, & 3 others to M[ts] 1760 besides the mony advanced to them	13	10	0
	Pd Dryden Sclaitor all work to the date p[r] disge	16	0	0
	Pd for 59 bolls meal to Dryden Gardiners & Work Serv[ts]	26	12	6
	Sume 1760	168	11	4

Note

(1) The Laird has left the quantity blank.

Discharge on Ale, Malt, Rum, Wine plate Meal &c 1760

		£	s	d
March	Pd Lord Erroll in full for Mountain Wine he sent to me	5	10	0
	Pd for 54 dozen of new bottles for Wine at Dryden	5	7	0
May	Pd James Stodert for Strong alle & small bear to Carnwath	10	0	0
	Pd Bell & Rannie for a hog[d] of Claret	32	14	0
	Pd Mr Hunter for 3 hog[ds] of strong alle & some small bear	7	1	2
	Pd D[d] Haig for Duty & making 31 bolls malt	5	14	10
	Pd Weir & Cochran for 31 bolls of barley	16	2	11
	Pd my plate Duty to	2	10	0

		£	s	d
July	Pd Mr McDougal for White wines post &c Pr Discharged Acct	87	0	0
Novr	Pd for meal to my family at Carnwath	3	11	8½
25	Pd James Stodert all ale & Whiskie furnished at Carnwath	2	14	0½
Decr 5	Pd for 43 bolls of meal toye date for my family since Decr 6 last year	19	0	9
	Sume 1760	97(1)	6	5

Note

(1) The Laird appears to have omitted to carry forward one hundred pounds, and although there is one entry which is rather smudged this could not possibly account for the discrepancy.

Discharge on my Children 1760

		£	s	d
May	Pd into Mr Fairholms acct for my Sons at Tubinguen &c (?)	400	0	0
	Pd (? ? ?) when was clear &c all our Accts	28	6	7
	both at Edinr & London by 2 fitted accounts when all was discharged	101	10	2
	Which I am to discharge and ? ? in different articles	529	16	9
Augt 29	Pd my sons Draught Feby 15 for 1759 100 Do May 29 for 1759 100 Sepr 1 for 1760 100 Decr 5 for 1759 125 March 8 for 1760 140 June 7 1760 145 £710 but having stated in 1759 accts £450 remitted to Mr Fairholm in London for my sons Draughts I am only now to charge him with the balance between that & the sume of his Draughts on me being	260	0	0
Augt 27	Pd Mr. Fairholme in London a Draught of my son James pr his bill from Vienna upon me (this is included in my clearance with Mr Fairholmes of this date) dated Jayr 8 1760	50	0	0
28	Pd my daughter her allowance at Whitsunday last	20	0	0
Novr 25	Pd my daughter her allowance at Marts pr advance	20	0	0

Dec[r]	1	Pd my son Charle by his own draught to Mr Couts	25 0 0
		Pd my Eldest sons Draughts by a bill sent to Mr. George Fairholme at London (of this Charle got £25) for	340 0 0
		Pd Mr Fairholme at Edin[r] for exchange on these bills	2 19 6
		Sume 1760	717 19 6

Here end my Accts for the year 1760

Note
Part of this page is almost illegible.

Discharge of Pocket mony 1761

Jay[r]	18	Pd Mrs. Lawson for a Rem of writing paper	12 0
		Pd my horses & Ser[vts] boats &c when my Daughter went to Dunibristle	10 6
	20	Pd all upsets Turnpikes boardwadges &c to the date	1 8 4
	23	Pd my subscription as a Hunter for the year 1761	5 5 0
		Pd for six packs of cards from Leith	5 0
		Pd my share of a Subscription ball at Walkers	1 17 0
Feby	7	Pd my livery Servants boardwadges & all accts to the date	1 7 0
	17	Spent in going & returning from Dunibristle	12 0
	18	Pd Mr Rae for drawing a tooth to me	5 0
		Pd Mr Smith for tuning the harpsicord till July 1760	1 1 0
March	2	Pd Doctor Clerk for attending me in a feaver £3=3 Mr Rattray for blooding & attendance 2=2	5 5 0
		Pd to a Collection for the Infirmary	1 1 0
		Pd Clerk for a case to my Magnifying Glass	5 0
	13	Pd my Serv[ts] upsets boardwadges &c to y[e] date	1 0 3
		Pd Mr Gordon for black paper	14 8
	17	Pd for ten Chairs & Window Curtains to Mr Pringle for Bristow house	24 0 0
		Pd for Stables horses & Serv[ts] at Leith races	2 1 8

May 13	Pd for Coach & Saddle horses at Leith races	1	15	0
	Pd for drinks to Carnwath people on Spots Victory	1	6	0
	Pd for 56 pound Coffee & a pound of tea a present to my Wife	5	1	0
	Pd Walter all triffles, accts, & boardwadges		9	6
	Given at Carnwath Kirk on my Daughters mariage	1	1	0
	Pd John Euart for going to Cassils with Minx's		7	6
	Pd for Coat rents(1) in Charity at Carnwath	1	0	0
	Pd George Stodert for writting my Bond to Lawrie Brown		10	6
May 30	Pd for Carstairs poor to Whity 1761		11	3
	Pd Dr Blair for attending Davie Lamb when ill		4	6
	Pd for making a black pulpit Cloath to Carnwath		2	6
	Pd for Cards from Glasgow	2	0	0
	Pd for Liberton poor to Lambas 1761		19	3½
June 4	Pd Thomas Sinclair for turnpikes, Servts, Ropes Tar &c &c	3	17	7
10	Pd for Wine at my Election President of the Archers	2	2	0
	Pd Mr Blansheill for a new furniture, two new briddles, Covering &c for my Daughters horse a present by me to her	4	3	8
	Pd for Drugs & attendance for Thos Borthwick & Wm Kelly when in feavers	1	1	0
22	Pd Upsets turnpikes & all my Livery Servts demands and Menzies accts to this date	3	13	10
	Pd for a headdress Ruffles &c a present to my Daughter	4	4	0
	Pd for a headdress &c to Miss Sinclair	2	2	0
	Pd Mr Rattray for a visit to me when ill at Dryden	1	1	0
July	Given Mr McKinning in Charity	2	2	0
	Pd at Clearing with the Clerks of the Royal Bank		5	0
	Pd Henderson for all pouder & lead shot to the date	1	12	0

		£	s	d
July 6	Pd for the Caledonian Mercury from July 1759 for advertisements to ye date per Mr Rudimans disge £5=2=0			
	Pd for the English newspapers to the date £5=2=9	10	4	9
	Pd Mr Bennett for all postages & his own trouble to the date	6	1	8
	Given my coaliers to drink on my birthday		10	6
	Given Charles Reid for keeping Spot in a present	1	1	0
	Pd Mr Robertson for a badge for the Musselburgh Arrow[(2)]		14	0
12	Pd Menzies accts Livery Servts &c turnpikes Upsets &c to the date	3	13[(3)]	4
	Pd Wm Kelly for Crows triffles &c		6	0
Sepr	Pd Mr Pringle for writing my Daughters Contract of Mariage	3	13	6
	Pd Mr Lawrie for some bottles of my cure agt Madness[(4)] pr acct Disged	1	18	0
	Pd Mr Rattray for coming to visit my Wife at Dryden	1	1	0
Oct 3	Pd for upsets boardwadges Oyle pouder &c to the date	3	8	0½
	Pd for letters at Biggar post office		10	8
	Pd for ane Entertainment to the Council of Lanark & some others who were in Capt Lockhart's [(5)] interest at his election	5	5	0
	Pd for a pound of red Sealing Wax		6	0
	Pd for pouder & lead to my Gardiners		8	0
	Pd for maintaining Carnwath poor to Marts 1761	2	16	4
Decr 10	Pd Mrs Lawson for 20 Quire writing paper		12	8
17	Pd George Stodert for assisting me at Marts		10	6
	Spent for Dinners to my Tennents at Paying their Marts rents	1	17	0
	Pd at Linton for beating[(6)] when returning to Dryden		4	0
	Pd Mr Bell to Marts 1761	10	0	0
	Pd for a wraping Gown a present to my Wife	1	5	6
	Pd Doctor Baillie for Drugs & attendance (in Ocr) to My Wife	2	2	0
	Sume 1761	£148	13	0[(7)]

Notes

(1) Coat rent—cot rent—cottage rent.
(2) The Musselburgh Arrow, a trophy competed for by the Royal Company of Archers.
(3) The figure is almost indecipherable.
(4) Cure against Madness; this may be connected in some way with the reference to the entry under June 13 1758 'Pocket Money', where money was paid for Drugs to cure 5 people bit by a mad dog.
(5) This may possibly be Thomas Lockhart's election to Parliament.
(6) Beating, betting is sometimes spelt in this way by the Laird but this does not make sense; perhaps it should read 'baiting' i.e. feeding the horses; Linton is now called West Linton and lies on the road from Carnwath to Dryden.
(7) The Laird made an error of £1.1.0. in his addition. The correct total should be £147.12.0.

Discharge on my Cloaths 1761

March 2d	Pd for 2 pair of mourning Gloves, & 2 pair black worsted stockings		15	0
	Pd for 2 neck silk handkerchiefs for hunting		10	0
June 5	Pd Mr Hope his acct due Marts last for things furnished to my wife & children	59	0	0
	Pd Mr Hercules all Cloaths made to ye date	4	15	0
	Pd Mr Blanshill for 2 black Velvet Hunting caps	2	10	0
	Pd for 2 hats to my self from Paris	1	14	0
	Pd for 4 pair worsted Stockings	1	2	0
Decr 24	Pd James Stodert for 2 pair hunting boots to my self	2	10	0
	Sume 1761	72	16	0

Discharge on my Stables, Horses, Hounds Coach &c 1761

Feby 7	Pd for breaking reins, a Swan's Skine,(1) for Spot, Phisick & Wm Graham's acct now payd		17	8
7	Pd Dryden Smith for Jany & former accts pr Disge	3	14	3
17	Pd for a boll of beans to Spot & Peg		10	0

March	Pd for brawn wheat & all Wm Grahames accts ropes for Spot &c		1	6	4
23	Pd Dryden Smith for Feby		1	13	9
May 13	Pd for booking Spot & Peg at Leith		2	12	0
	Pd Lord Eglinton's Groom for winning with Spot		3	3	0
	Pd my Grooms boardwadges & triffles at Leith with Spot & Peg		2	11	6
	Pd Bailie Wilson for Hay & beans to Spot & Peg Litter &c		1	17	6
	Pd Wm Grahame for my hunters and him self at Leith		1	2	4
	Pd for plating Spot & Peg JS			10	0
	Pd James Stodert for a Clogbag(2) horse		8	0	0
June 1	Pd Carnth Shoemaker for all repairs to Harness &c pr disged Accts		1	16	10
	Pd Wm Grahame for hoove salve all saddles repaired &c			13	3
	Pd Thos Jackson for attending the Dogs			16	6
	Pd for 16 bolls Dog meal to Carnwath		6	0	6
	Pd all my Carnth tennents for Corne Straw furnished to my Stables preceeding this date being 100 bolls, 11 pecks in all received from them		52	4	8
	Pd for Hay to my Cattle last winter at Shodshill		2	3	4
	Pd John Weir for Hay Crop 1760	£23			
	Pd Wm Cochran for do	£33	56	0	0
	Pd Weir, Aitken, & Mitchell for 69 bolls, 8 pecks, Corn & Straw		40	10	10
	Pd Dryden Smith for March April & May		4	5	7
5	Sent to Mr Fairholme at London on a bill to pay my mare Pegs price stated as payd in 1760 in my accts		£24–7–6		
20	Pd Spot & his keepers Expences in Fife		2	7	0
	Pd Mr Blanshill for Girths, Repairs, Flannell &c per disged to the date		2	1	4
	Pd Jack Smith Some wadges due to him ere he left my service in full		3	6	8
	Pd Grant all repairs about my Saddles to the date			5	0
	Pd for Candles to Dryden Stables to the date			13	0

July 15	Pd ane old acct Wighting (?) Servts at Leith & for Spots & Pegs riders		12	6
	Pd Purdie all horse Drugs to the date for Dogs &c &c		11	10
	Pd Dryden Smith for June & July	3	9	0
	Pd my Coach & chaise duty to April 1762	6	0	0
Sepr	Pd Mr. Blanshill all work & repairs to my saddles to the date		18	0
	Pd Thos Sinclair for 7 bolls of Dog meal to Dryden	3	9	8
	Pd Dryden Smith for Augt & Sepr	2	11	4
	Pd Wm Grahame for 4 bolls of Brawn £00–10–6 for hoove Salve £00–10–6 for Ropes Drugs Turnpikes 3–9[3]	1	3	9
October	Pd Charles Reid his expences in going with Peg to Perth & in his returning home boardwadges turnpikes boats &c	3	5	0
Novr	Pd James Clerk his wadges to Marts 1761 for breeding Bella & Sancho & for meal for these to Dogs when with him in full	4	0	6
	Pd for 27 bolls Dog meal bought in Augt last	13	16	9
	Pd Hugh Smith & Thos Brown for 23 bolls of oats to Carnth	10	10	0
	Pd all straw bought for Carnwath Stables to the date	5	10	0
	Pd Jas Wallace all Smith work at Carnth to the date	6	0	0
	Pd John Nimmo all repairs to horses & Servts Cloaths to ye date		17	0
	Pd John Scott for repairs to Boots Harnes &c Pr disged act		16	0
	Pd Doctor Blair for all horse Drugs to the date	1	3	8
	Pd Andw Smith for farrier work & Drugs to the date		9	0
	Pd Carnth Couper to the date		4	10
	Pd Lanark Saidler to the date		6	4

Nov^r	Pd George Aitken for 26 bolls Oats sent in July to Dryden	12	7	0
	Pd Dryden Smith for October & Nov^r	2	12	8
	Pd in Augt for a black Hunter (Monky) from Mr. Beale	30	0	0
Decr 8	Pd for 32 bolls Dog meal bought for Dryden	16	0	0
	Pd John Stodert for 20 bolls Dog meal laid up for Spring hunting	10	0	0
	Pd Thomas Jackson all due for his attending the Dogs		15	0
	Sume 1761	£248	11	10

Notes

(1) Swan's Skine—Swan's skin: a soft twilled flannel.
(2) Clogbag—saddlebag.
(3) The extension of this entry is a shilling too little.

Discharge on My Servants Cloaths Wadges &c 1761

March 2	Pd for Mournings to Mrs Kerr when my Eldest Son died		2	0	0
	Pd Thomas Borthwick in part of his wadges p^r advance		1	1	0
May 13	Pd George Montgomery for Wadges & Dyet whilst with me		1	13	0
18	Pd Walter Taylor, George Clarihew & John Euart their wadges in full		9	6	0
June	Pd Wm Grahame all repairs for saddles, Hoove salve &c to the date		–	0	0
	Pd Thos Jackson for attending the Kennel at Carnwath		–	0	0
	Pd Mr Smart for 20 yards blew Cloath for Serv^ts Cloaths		9	10	0
	Pd my Postilion in part of his Wadges	£1–			
	Pd Wm Montgomery in part of his Wadges	15			
	Pd Thos Borthwick in part of his Wadges	£1..1			
	Pd Wm Kelly in part of his Wadges	£2..2			
	Pd Js Purdie in part of his Wadges	£1..1	5	19	0
	Pd Dryden Taylor all work to the date for Serv^ts Liverys &c &c		5	8	0

July	Pd for six hats from Holland to my Servants	3	3	0
	Pd Mrs Lawson for Shirts to Dd Lamb		11	1
	Given my Postilion more to account of his Wadges		4	0
Nov^r	Pd Menzies his Wadges to Mart^s 1761	7	0	0
	Pd Anthony Dixon d^o to M^s 1761	3	10	0
	Pd Peter Sinclair d^o to M^s 1761	2	10	0
Decr 5	Pd Ja^s Stodert Wm Grahame, Wm Kelly Jas Purdie Will Montgomery Charles Reid, Thos Borthwick & my postilion in full with former payments of their Wadges to Marts 1761	52	16	0
	Pd Thos Cuthbertson for cloaths to Wm Montgomery		15	0
	Pd for meal to my Grooms at Carn^th to M 1761	2	11	6
10	Pd for 2 pair of Stockings to Davie Lamb £00–5 3 handkerchiefs to Do 3 a velvet cap to Do 15	1	3	0
	Sume 1761	£109	0	7

Discharge on Miscellanys books building Ditching Labouring &c 1761

Jay^r 18	Pd for trenching the avenue thorn hedges at Dryden	1	8	0
	Pd for trenching 112 roods of Rosline avenue for potatoes	3	14	8
	Pd the Earl of Aboyne for 4 pounds of fir seed		10	0
June 1	Pd Spence for new Windows, repairs, paint, & all work to the date	2	13	0
	Pd Lanark Glazier all work to the date		9	0
	Pd Monylas for sawing building repairs Quarry work &c to ye date	10	8	0
	Pd Thos Mitchell for a pair of Cart Wheels	1	0	0
	Pd Ja^s Cleland for Locks, kees, ? , &c p^r disged acct	1	10	11
	Pd Dryden Days Wadges men to June 1st 1761	4	8	0
8	Pd Alexander Brown for grinding Victual to ye date		11	8

June 8	Pd the mole catcher at Dryden to the date		8	4
	Pd Mr Rainnie for Iron furnished to Dryden to the date p[r] disge	4	11	0
	Pd Aikman, Hunter & Hall, in part of their Wadges	4	10	0
	Pd for covering again all Dryden Windows & for new Painting 3 rooms	5	11	0
8	Pd Dryden Coupar for 12 new iron tubs &c for my Orange Trees	2	3	0
	Pd for keeping Dryden Windows to Wy 1761 for cleaning for new windows to the stair head Room &c &c £3	4	10	0
Sep 1	Pd Dryden Days Wadges men to the last of July	3	10	8
	Pd for mowing Dryden Hay	1	17	4
	Pd for weeding Dryden nurserys		8	4
	Pd for new nets to Dryden fruit trees		18	0
	Pd James Blackie for 3 new Windows & all repairs to Dryden	7	0	0
	Pd for cutting winning & Inning Dryden Fearns	2	10	6
	Pd Dryden Days Wadges men for Aug[t]	1	4	8
	Pd for inning Dryden Hay		18	4
	Pd D[d] Macklaren for casting the front of Dryden house	1	1	4
	Pd D[d] Macklaren for jobs at Bristow & Carnwath house		8	2
Nov 23	Pd for Coals Cariage Ale to Carnwath house	4	15	8
	Pd J[n] Stodert for mowing winning & inning Carnwath hay crop	5	16	11
	Pd James Paterson for Ropes Nails &c per Disge		13	9
	Pd John Walker all Cariages to Marts 1761	2	1	8
	Pd Will[m] Spence all Wright Work to the date	1	9	0
	Pd George Baine all Smith work to Carnwath house	1	14	2
	Pd Carnwath Massons in full to the date	1	1	6
	Pd Purdie for upholding Carnwath roof to the date Sclates Nails &c		10	0
	Pd Ormiston & Crawford their mony wadges to Mart[s] 1761	6	0	0

		£	s	d
Decr	Pd Dryden Gardiner & 3 Lads their Wadges to Marts 1761	11	0	0
	Pd Thos Sinclair Robt Aikman, Robt Lind Dd Hunter & Wm Hall to Mts 1761	15	10	0
	Pd for sawing all deals at Dryden to the date	3	1	10
	Pd Jas Monylas all Masson work at Dryden to the date	2	14	7
	Pd Thos Sinclair for Custome Ropes Tar &c to the date	3	0	11
	Pd for Shearing Dryden Crop	2	4	3
Decr 1761	Pd Dryden 2 hired men for October & Novr	4	2	0
	Pd Jas Gibson for Drugs & attendance on the Cows to the date		12	6
	Pd for 14 bolls of Lime to Dryden house from Brughlee		14	0
	Pd for meal to Grahame Ormiston & Crawford to Marts 1761	10	11	3
	Pd for meal to Dryden Gardiners Grieve & Work Servts (85 bolls 8p)	31	13	9
	Pd Jas Cleland for a new Chimney back & all work at Dryden	2	7	0
	Pd Jn Stodert for cutting & inning Shodshill Hay	1	11	2
8	Pd John Lockhart for sawing fire wood	1	0	0
	Pd Charle Borthwick & the Herds Wife for all work to the date		10	6
	Pd for Saugh Slips & Cariages from Stobo		3	6
	Sume 1761	£183	13	10

Note

The Laird's total is almost illegible.

Discharge on Ale Malt Rum Wine Plate Meal &c 1761

		£	s	d
May	Pd for fruit & Sugar for punch	4	0	0
June 1	Pd James Stodert for ale to Carnwath to the date	11	12	6
	Pd Wier & Cochran for 32 bolls of Barley	16	8	0
	Pd Dd Haig for malting 48 bolls of Barley from Old Liston & Rosline	7	18	8
	Pd Mr Brunton to acct of Wine delivered by him to me	8	0	0

			£	s	d
June	1	Pd Mr Brunton to deliver to Mr Gordon a Guinea (which he did not do) & must now be charged to part pay[t] of Wine delivered to me	1	1	0
		Pd for 7 bolls meal from Dalkeith to Dryden family	3	9	8
Dec[r]	5	Pd Ja[s] Stodert for alle & spirits to Carnwath house to the date	12	15	8
		Pd for meal to Carnwath house to Ms 1761	8	16	8
		Pd for meal to Carnwath house to M[s] 1761	24	15	7
		Sume 1761	£98	17	9

Discharge on my Children 1761

			£	s	d
June	5	Pd Mr. Fairholme at Edin[r] to acct for my son Charles Draughts	90	0	0
		Sent Mr Fairholme at London to answer my son James last Draught	100	0	0
July	15	Pd Mr Fairholme in London all his demands for my eldest sons books or draughts or any other thing, for Jamies bills from Vienna, Rollm(1) & London, for Comm[n], postages & interest, being all due to him p[r] Disged Accts. the mony now remitted by his brothers bills being in full	122	18	1
Aug[t]		Pd Charle in a present towards a hunter	20	0	0
Dec[r]		Pd Charle to acc[t] of his allowance between Wy & Marts	30	0	0
		Pd Mr Fairholme in full of Charles Bills Interest & Exchange	23	8	7
		Given Charle in a present	10	0	0
		Pd Mr Fairholme in part of £300 ordered from Whity 1761 to Whity 1762 for my son James pr his receipt	150	0	0
	10	Pd to the faculty of Advocates at my son Charles privat Tryalls for passing Advocate	40	0	0
		Sume 1761	£586	6	8

Here end my Acc[ts] for 1761

Note

(1) This abbreviation is not easily identified. Perhaps it refers to Rotterdam and the Laird did not cross the t's.

Discharge Pocket Mony 1762

Jayr	Pd John Medina for stenting (?) & cleaning some Pictures[(1)]	1	1	0
	Pd Charles Congleton for blooding my Wife		10	6
	Pd ane Express to Kelso (with the 3d extract) to overtake Capt Gordon		11	6
	Pd my subscription as a Hunter for the year 1762	5	5	0
	Pd for being absent from the Perth meeting 1761	1	1	0
	Pd ane Entertainment to ye Archers Council at Signing Jamies Commission	1	3	0
	Lost this winter at play & spent in my pocket Chair plays &c	25	15	0
Feby	Given in Charity to the Infirmary	1	1	0
14	Pd Doctor Clerk for attending on me £3.3 Charles Congleton bleeding &c £1.1	4	4	0
	Pd the Dues of Coll Lockharts Commn as ane Officer of the Archers	2	12	6
	Pd Mrs. Drummond for a good Clock	4	4	0
March 15	Given in Charity		10	6
	Pd Jas Somers for recovering two guineas I had given Wm Ramage		5	0
	Pd Mr Robertson for writing Articles of Charle's Mariage with Miss Macdonald	1	1	0
22	Pd Henry D'larche my Servts expences for turnpikes, for powder, oyle, brushes, shovels, Ribbands, (A Crown to ye pipe watter keeper for 1762) board wadges &c &c	6	0	5
April 12	Spent in Edinr		15	0
May 29	Spent in my pocket at Carnwath found (?) Horses (?) &c	1	1	0
	Pd Carnwath Clock maker to Whity 1762		2	6
	Pd Liberton poors maintenance to Lambas 1762	1	8	11
	Pd for upholding & repairing my fishing net to Whity 1762		15	0
June 9	Pd my 3d share of expences in bringing home & wanting (?) of Essence[(2)]	1	10	0

			£	s	d
June	9	Pd my 3d Share of Mr Wicks bill for 30 bottles of Essence	10	10	0
		Pd Mr Fairholme at Edin^{r} all his demands on me in full		1	4
		Pd Thomas Sinclair for turnpikes Tar Ropes &c to Wy 1762	3	7	10
	22	Pd all my Grooms for turnpikes boardwadges triffles &c to ye date	2	16	0
		Pd for a pound of tea a present to Mrs Kerr		6	0
	29	Pd the Fiddlers who came to Dryden for dancing	1	10	0
		Given my coaliers for to drink on my birthday		10	0
July	5	Pd for a Gown a present to my Wife	12	13	6
	8	Pd Henry Larche for turnpikes boardwadges oyle pouder & all my Serv^{ts} demands	5	11	3½
		Pd all eatables when at Carnwath		10	0
	17	Pd Mr Henderson for all Gunpowder & Shot to the date	1	10	0
August	9	Given Charles towards the price of a new hunter	5	0	0
	26	Spent for eatables when at Carnwath 2^{ce} this summer	1	2	0
Sep^{r}	4	Spent in my Journy to Biddleston & return from Mr Selby	2	5	0
		Pd Mr Finlayson for a picture of Mrs Gordon to my Wife	7	17	6
	11	Pd for my horses & Servants at Calendar (turnpikes &c)	1	18	6
	28	Pd for my familys Expences at Carnwath by Henry's accts	1	12	0
Oct^{r}	15	Given some poor people at Carnwath		8	0
Oct^{r}	22	Pd for a mare a present by me to John Stodert	1	1	0
		Pd Mr Henderson all Gun pouder & Shot to the date	1	1	0
	27	Pd James Stodert for some Sheets of stamped paper		10	6

		£	s	d
Nov[r]	Pd George Montgomery for my Tennents dinner & some other dinners to Tennents, Punch to them &c &c	2	14	0
	Pd George Stodert for assisting me when receiving my Rents[(3)]		10	6
	Pd for expresses & triffles & Cariage of Madaira from Glasgow	1	0	6
Dec[r] 20	Pd Mrs Lawson all mony laid out for me to this date		10	6
	Pd my Grooms & Coachman all acc[ts] for upsets boardwadges turnpikes brawn Oyle brushes phisick &c &c Expences &c	4	9	0
	Pd Henry L'arche his acc[ts] for Serv[ts] & triffles to the date	4	12	0
30	Pd the hire of 42 carts loaded with Coals to Bristow house	6	1	8
	Pd my wood cutters for 2 large ash trees to be left growing by them, the one near the Lee quarry the other near the Gardiners		14	0
	Pd for Drinks to 4 boys & to my beagles by Mr Lawries Disge	1	11	3
	Pd Bristow house Gate keeper in a Compliment for 1762		15	0
	Spent when in Edin[r] at Christmas		15	6
	Pd for a Gold head to a Cane a present to Mrs Pringle	3	7	6
	Pd for setting a seal that belonged to my Eldest Son	2	0	0
	Pd Mr Bell to Marts 1762	10	0	0
	Pd to Carnwath poors maintenance	5	0	0
	Sume 1762	166	0	8[(4)]

Notes

(1) Medina—Sir John Medina the well known portrait painter who painted several pictures of the 18th century Lockharts. For 'stenting' perhaps stretching is a possible answer.

(2) Essence—perhaps some flavouring, or a cosmetic.

(3) George Stodert for assisting me—this was probably a son of James Stodert the factor. It may be inferred from this entry that the Hunting Laird collected his own rents, and generally managed his own estate, always remembering that the greater part of the estate was let on Tack to his brother Alexander.

(4) The total should be £167.0.08.

	Discharge on my Cloaths 1762			
Feby	Pd for six cotton caps to my self		12	0
March	Pd Jas Stodert for shoes & spurs		8	0
June 23	Pd for 6 pieces of Stocking for a Waistcoat & breatches to my Self	1	12	6
	Pd for 6 under Cotton Caps		7	0
Ocr 15	Pd Mr John Hope his acct for Cloaths to my Wife & me (by bill payble at Marts 1763) in full of all I owe pr Dischged acct	77	9	0
	Pd Mr Scott in full for my Cloaths to ye date by my bill payable Marts 1763 per disged acct	27	8	0
Decr 31	Pd Hercules for making my Cloaths pr disged acct to the date	4	0	0
	Sume 1762	£112	16	6[1]

Note
(1) The Laird's total is a pound too much.

1762	**Discharge on Stables Horses Hounds Coach &c 1762**			
Jyr 6	Pd Gardiner ferrier[1] for all Drugs & attendance to the date disge	6	10	0
	Pd Mr Hume all Coach & harnass work pr Disged acct	5	0	0
	Pd Mr Thomson for 9 bolls of pease to my horses	4	3	4
	Pd Dryden Smith for Decr & Jany last all work	3	8	2
	Pd for booking & Riding Peg at Leith race	3	7	0
March	Pd Mr Ferrier for oat Straw for litter to my horses at Bristow house	1	5	9
22	Pd for 8 bolls of Dog meal to Dryden of this date	4	0	0
	Pd for a hunting Whip to Will Montgomery		4	6
	Pd Dryden Smith for Febry & March	3	8	4½
	Pd for a little mare for riding with my Servts &c	4	4	0
	Pd John Stodert for a Work horse for Carnwath	7	0	0

May 30	Pd Hugh Smith Jas Somerville & others for 78 bolls of Corn & Straw	48	17	9
	Pd John Weir George Aitken Widow Bowars & Thomas Mitchell for 108 bolls of Corn & the Straw sold to me at Dryden in all	63	5	10
June 9	Pd John Weir Wm Cochran & David Wilson for Hay Crop 1761	0	0	0
	Pd John Weir & Wm Cochran for 32 bolls of barley	0	0	0
	Pd John Weir for his hay Crop 1761 £22–1 Wm Cochran for Do £25–16 David Wilson for Do £28–17	76	14	0
	Pd for 8 bolls of Dog meal to Dryden	5	4	0
	Pd Thos Jackson for attending the Beagles last Spring		12	0
	Pd my Grooms for Brawn Oyle, briddles, brushes, Candles &c	4	0	2
	In this acct 3 lanthorns are included			
July 5	Pd for a young Coach Gelding	13	13	0
Augt 5	Pd my Coach & Chaise duty to April 1763	6	0	0
	Pd George Thomson for 2 bolls 8 pecks of pease & beans	1	2	6
	Pd for 16 bolls north country meal to my Dogs	8	16	0
Sepr 6	Pd for booking Spot at Leith £1–6/- Pd Mr Kers Groom for riding Spot 3–3/-	4	9	0
	Pd Charles Reid all expences with Spot at Leith & going with him to England & bring home my 2 horses I got in exchange for him	2	3	3
Novr	Pd for 56 bolls Corn & Straw bought in June from my tennents	39	1	11
	Pd John Scott for litter furnished to my horses	2	11	0
	Pd James Wallace for a years shoeing pr disge	8	12	0
	Pd Lanark Saidler for all repairs to the date		16	0
	Pd Lanark Saidler for a new watering Saddle	1	1	0
	Pd Dr Blair for triffles to my horses to the date		6	5
	Pd Wm Dalyell for 20 bolls 8 p Oats to my horses at Dryden	12	9	5

			£	s	d
D	2	Pd Dryden Smith to the date	9	12	0
		Pd Chrighton Coachmaker for a new Post Chaise for painting harness &c pr disged acct	60	18	0
		Pd Mr Lock for 48 bolls of dog meal to Dryden	28	2	6
		Pd Rosline for Hay sent to Edinr	12	10	0
		Pd Rosline for Wheat straw sent to Dryden	20	0	0
		Pd Thomas for attending my Dogs at Carnwath		11	2
	27	Pd Mr Blenchill for pannels stuffing repairs & pr Disge	3	18	0
		Sume 1762	477	18	0(2)

Notes

(1) Perhaps farrier.

(2) The Laird failed to include the half penny.

Discharge on my Servts Cloaths Wadges &c 1762

			£	s	d
Jayr	6	Pd Mr Thomson all breatches to my Servts to the date	3	2	0
March	22	Pd for leather breatches of this date to Wm Montgomery & my Postilion		11	0
		Pd James Coupar in full when he left my Service		3	6
		Pd my new Postilion per advance to buy necessaries	1	12	8
		Pd Carnth Shoemaker for boots & repairs to the date	1	9	0
		Pd Wm Kelly in part of his Wadges due Marts 1762	2	0	0
		Pd Thos Borthwick in part of his Wadges due Marts 1762	2	0	0
		Pd Alexr Scot when he left my Service in full of Wadges	4	0	0
		Pd Dryden Taylor in full of making & repairing Cloaths to ye date	3	12	0
June	23	Pd John Scot in full of his Wadges to Marts 1762 pr advance	7	0	0
		Pd for Cloath for my Livery Servts by Mr Smarts acct & discharge	9	10	0

		£	s	d
July 8	Pd Henry Larche to account of his years Wadges due at Mart^s^ 1762	3	0	0
15	Pd Charles Reid all Wadges or demands on any Acc^t^ to this date	6	10	0
19	Pd Will Montgomery to acc^t^ of his Wadges due Mart^s^ next		15	0
	Pd for Glass windows broke by John Scot & David in part of their wadges		4	0
Novr 27	Pd James Clerk his Wadges to Mart^s^ 1762	1	0	0
	Pd John Nimmo & John Tweedale for repairs to my Serv^ts^		11	6
	Pd Cuthbertson for course Cloath for my Serv^ts^ p^r^ diged Acc^t^	5	12	6
	Pd John Scot Shoemaker for repairs		8	2
	Pd James Stodert his Wadges to M 1762 £25			
	Pd more to Henry Larche in full to M 1762 £12			
	Pd Wm Grahame & Purdie in full to D^o^ £14			
	Pd more to Wm Kelly & T Borthwick to D^o^ £10			
	Pd more to Montgomery & Postilion to D^o^ £2–15/-			
	Pd David Wilson half a year to D^o^ £4	67	15	0
	Sume 1762	£120	16	4

Discharge on Miscellanys Building Ditching Labouring Gardings, Books &c 1762

		£	s	d
Jay^r^ 30	Pd for enclosing William Murrays farm at Dryden	5	3	0
Feby 18	Pd for enclosing Widdow Ainsleys farm at Dryden	4	9	3
	Pd Dryden Days Wadges men for Dec^r^ & Jay^r^ last	2	16	8
	Pd Thos Mitchell for 2 pair of Cart Wheels for Carnwath	2	0	0
	Pd Dryden Days Wadges men for Feby	2	18	8
	Pd Dryden Smith for Shoeing Cart Wheels for Carnwath	1	0	10
	Pd for making up the Kennel into a Stable at Carnwath	1	0	0

		£	s	d
May 29	Pd Lanark Glazier all work at Carnwath to the date		1	3
	Pd for making a fold for Carnwath moss band Cattle		18	0
	Pd for 272 load of Coals to Carnwath house to the date Carriage alle &c	3	19	4
	Pd John Kelly & Others for planting &c at Carnwath	3	2	8
	Pd for new Cart Saddles, Breatchings Girthing &c		18	6
	Pd Wm Spence for making Gates, cutting firs & many Triffles		15	6
	Pd John Stodert to advance for Dung bought for the new parks	4	0	0
	Pd George Baine for new locks, kees &c pr Disged Acct		15	0
June 9	Pd Dryden Days Wadges men for May & preceedings	5	1	4
	Pd Dryden Smith for April & May	1	10	11
	Pd Dryden Gardiner for weeding for bee scapes &c		9	8
	Pd James Monylas for Sawing Fir trees &c to the date	4	16	4
	Pd Alexr Brown for grinding Grotts(1) meal &c to the date		15	10
	Pd Robt Linds Wife for herding to the date		15	0
	Pd for keeping Dryden Windows in repair to Wy 1762	1	10	0
	Pd James Monylas for Jobs Days work repairs &c to June 1st	1	19	10
July 21	Pd for new pottying all Dryden windows		13	6
	Pd Robt Aikman, Dd Hunter, & Wm Hall in part of their Wadges due Ms 1762	6	0	0
	Pd my Coaliers for carrying deals from Brughlee Saw pit		10	0
Novr 27	Pd for a Ditch & dead hedge to preserve my trees from Mr Christie		17	6
	Pd James Cleland for Work, new bolts bands Locks &c Pr disged acct	3	3	0
	Pd for 340 loads of Coals, Cariage Ale, for peets &c to Carnwath house	6	0	2

Novr 27	Pd for cutting winning & inning Carnwath Hay	4	5	4
	Pd for cutting down a Crop I bought at Greenalltown	3	14	6
	Pd Archd Prentice for Wheat Thack, for Carnth, offices, Workmanship	2	13	6
	Pd Dung gathering Stones, cutting rashes, filling Dung Spreading &c &c about Carnwath new park	6	8	3
	Pd for new Sacks to Carnwath & Dryden	1	8	0
	Pd Wm Spence all wright work to the date pr disge	2	10	0
	Pd James Paterson for Ropes Tar &c &c pr disge	1	7	5
	Pd George Bean for 5 new Gate Locks & triffles to ye date	1	8	11
	Pd Wm Walker all Cariages to the date		19	4
	Pd Carnwath massons all triffles & repairs		13	10
	Pd James Purdie for upholding Carnwath house Roof & for some jobs to the date		14	0
27	Pd Ormiston & Crawford a years mony Wadges to M 1762	6	0	0
	Pd Gilchrist & Montgomery half a years Wadges to M 1762	3	15	0
	Pd my Gardiners, Thos Sinclair, & Dryden Servts in full to M 1762	25	0	0
	Pd Dryden hired men for June July & Augt Sepr Octr & Novr	12	16	8
	Pd for winning & inning Dryden Ferns	1	4	10
	Pd for Shearing Dryden Crop	2	1	8
	Pd for thatching Dryden Offices, Haystack Ferns &c	2	1	0
Decr 1	Pd Thos Sinclair for custom ropes Tar &c all due to the date	3	7	0
	Pd John Hunter & John Harper for Wheat Straw	4	15	6
	Pd Mr Richard for 59 bolls of Lime for casting Dryden house	3	11	3
	Pd my herds wife in full for herding		11	4
	Pd James Monylas all work at Dryden to the date	3	18	4
	Pd James Mack for 2 new plows to Carnwath	3	18	4

Dec[r] 1	Pd for a years meal to Dryden Gardiners (26B)	18 17 9
	Pd for a years meal to my whole Dryden Work Serv[ts](32B 8p)	23 12 6
	Sume 1762	209 16 0

Note
(1) Perhaps groats or coarse grain.

Discharge on Ale Malt Rum Wine Plate Meal 1762

Jay[r] 18	Pd for 2 Chests of Lemonds for Punch	7 0 0
June	Pd James Stodert for strong & Small alle to Carnwath	11 0 0
	Pd Mr Ridock factor for Rob[t] Brunton all Wine furnished to me	42 7 7
	Pd John Weir & W[m] Cochran for 32 bolls Barley for Malt	16 16 0
	Pd David Haig for malting 48 bolls of Barley (Duty &c)	6 12 8
	Pd D[d] Haig for 36 Gallons of ale to Dryden house	1 16 0
	Pd Mr Maccara for Rum to Dryden	4 13 0
	Pd my Tax for plate to July 5 1763	2 15 0
Nov[r] 20	Pd James Wallace for ten pints of Rum	1 13 4
Nov[r] 27	Pd W[m] Telfer for 2 anchors of Rum	6 0 0
	Pd Mr Bogle at Glasgow for half a pipe of Madaira	32 11 1
	Pd James Stodert all ale to my family at Carnwath	9 8 0
	Pd Mr Macdougals heirs for 2 hogd[s] Wine & interest p[r] discharged Acc[t] to the date	43 16 0
	Pd Mr Ross for 2 hogd[s] white wine, for Rum Port &c pr disged acct to the date	57 12 0
	Pd for 55 bolls, 8 pecks of meal bought & from Carnwath & Oldliston to my family at Dryden to Decr 1762	39 8 9
	Sume 1762	£283 9 5

Discharge on my Children 1762

		£	s	d
Jay[r] 4	Given Capt Gordon[1] to pay a bill of Jamies to Mr Fairholme London	100	0	0
	Pd Charle in part of his allowance from Marts 1761 to Wy 1762	25	0	0
	Sent to Mr Fairholme at London by his Brothers bills £100 to pay the said sume taken up by Capt Gordon to buy horses for General Loudon & Jamie	100	0	0
	Pd Mr Fairholme the Exchange on the said bill	3	15	0
	Pd Mr Fairholme in full my Som Jamies Allowance from Wy 1761 to Wy 1762	150	0	0
	Pd my son Charles from Mart[s] to Wy 1762 now & formerly in full	25	0	0
June 30	Pd Mr Fairholmes a bill of my son Jamies from Vienna	200	0	0
	Lent my Son James by a draught on Glasgow Bank	25	0	0
	Pd Mr Fairholme in full of my son James Allowance to M 1762	150	0	0
	Pd Mr & Mrs Gordon in full of Annt[s] due M 1762	00	0	0
	Pd Charles Lockhart in full of Annt[s] & Annuity to M 1762	00	0	0
	Pd my son James in advance to W 1763	50	0	0
	Sume 1762	£828	15	0

My acct[s] end here for the year 1762

Note

(1) Captain Gordon: the Laird's cousin and son-in-law, he married Clementina Lockhart in 1761. Jamie: the Laird's second son serving in the army of Maria Theresa, Empress of Austria. General Loudon was another Scot serving the Empress.

Discharge Pocket Mony 1763

		£	s	d
Jay[r] 10	Pd my Annual Payment as a Hunter for 1763	5	5	0
	Pd for being absent from the meeting at Kelso	1	1	0
12	Spent in the taverns &c at Edin[r]	2	2	0
22	Spent in going & coming from Dunibirsle		10	0

		£	s	d
Jay[r] 31	Pd for digging a Hunted fox		10	6
	Pd D[r] Hutchinson for attendance at Dryden	1	1	0
Feb[y] 4	Pd for translating my son James's patent Creating him a Barron	2	2	0
24	Pd for Garnets a present to my Daughter Cara(1)	1	12	6
March 3	Pd Lord Erroll a beat lost at Leith	6	6	0
	Spent in my Pocket during the winter for all triffles	12	12	0
10	Pd Mr Balfours Children for a Snuff box		14	0
	Pd Ormiston all triffles he ever did for me		3	0
	Pd for Stamped paper & expences 3 times at Linton		18	2
	Pd for ane express to the Isle of Man(2)	1	11	6
May	Pd W[m] Kelly for all Earths Stop't to the date		8	0
	Pd for keeping Carnwath Clocks to Wy 1763		2	6
	Pd for upholding Carnwath fishing nett to Wy 1763		15	0
	Pd Alex[r] Brown his loss by the turnpike road to W 1763		10	0
	Pd Ja[s] Stodert his expences in my business to the date	1	16	8
	Pd Ja[s] Stodert & Mrs Lawson for 2 pound red wax		12	0
	Pd Mr Fleming all advertisement to the date	1	18	0
	Pd Dr Hutchinson for bleeding & attendance		15	6
	Pd Henry for all turnpikes, boardwadges pounder oyle &c pr acc[t] disgd	5	1	4
June	Pd for a dinner & musick to my Coaliers on my birthday	1	16	6
	Pd Mrs Lawson for half a Rime of Paper		10	0
July	Spent for boats & going & coming from Dunibirstle		10	0
Aug[t]	Spent for 10 Days eating at Carnwath, to Dr Sanders Charity to W[m] Liddle for trouble &c	2	18	0
	Pd for a Cow from Biddleston a present to my Daughter	4	9	4
	Advanced Henry Larche to account	3	3	0
	Pd for expences taking Doos(3) at Yester &c &c	1	10	0

Augt	Pd all postages at Edr & letters cariers to Sepr 1763	6	0	7
	Pd for some prints from Espline for Carnwath		8	0
	Pd Mr Row for taying[(4)] 2 teeth for me		10	0
	Pd one years Subscription to the Manaye at Edr	10	10	0
	Pd Wm Mackye for a parcil of Quighs[(5)]	1	0	0
	Pd George Montgomery for my tennents Dinners Novr 1763	2	0	0
	Pd for Red Hose[(6)], A Saddle, a pair of Shoes, for races after Carnwath Fair	1	5	6
	Pd for Drugs to Wm Kelly & Dd Sanderson by Dr Mickles disged Acct		11	0
	Pd Mrs Lawson for a rime of paper		12	8
	Pd for maintaining Liberton poor to Augt 1763		15	3
	Pd Joshua Johnston for cards formerly sent to me	5	7	5
	Pd Mr Fairholme all postages due his brother in London	9	7	1
	Pd for 2 hats to James & Charles Brothwick		3	8
	Pd Mr Rattray & Congleton for all Drugs bloodings &c	6	6	4
	Pd Robt Lin for Crows & ale to Earth Stoppers		2	8
	Pd Henry Larche in full for Servts boardwadges for turnpikes Oyle paper pouder pr acct disged	1	11	1
	Pd for all eatables at Carnwath in Sepr		14	2
	Advanced Henry Larche to account	1	0	0
	Pd Mr Rudiman for News papers & all advertisements to October 5 1763	5	8	0
	Pd Mr Row for putting a false tooth in to me	1	1	0
	Spent in Edr		10	6
	Pd Mrs Lawson for a handkerchief & gilded writing paper		10	10
	Pd Henderson all Gunpouder to the date	1	2	0
	Given Mr Gordon my mare Cattain (?) (Sold by him for £21)	21	0	0
	Given Mrs Gordon a Grey filly well worth 15 Guineas	15	15	0

		£	s	d
Aug[t]	Given my son Charle my horse blott for a Stalion at Cara[(7)]	5	5	0
	Pd Mr Bell to Mart[s] 1763	10	0	0
	Pd Liberton poor for Charity to M 1763	3	0	0
	1763 Sume	£175	2	3

Notes

(1) 'My daughter Cara'; there is no record of any daughter of this name, perhaps it was a nickname.
(2) The Laird's brother, William, made his home in the Isle of Man after he was court-martialled and dismissed from the Army.
(3) Doos—doves or pigeons.
(4) Taying, this is probably taking i.e. extracting.
(5) Quighs—Quicks i.e. Thorns.
(6) The estate of Carnwath is still held from the Crown under a Blench Duty of One Pair of Red Hose to be the prize for the winner of a foot race to be run annually.
(7) The 'Cara' referred to here is probably the island of that name off the West Coast of Kintyre and part of the Estate of Largie which came into the possession of Charles Lockhart on his marriage to the heiress Elizabeth Macdonald in 1762.

Discharge on my Cloaths 1763

		£	s	d
March 24	Pd Mr Smith all Gloves furnished me to the date		19	6
	Pd Mrs Lawson for 8 pair under stockings	1	7	10
	Pd Mr Gordon for 2 hats bought for my self	2	10	0
	Pd Mr Smart for Cloath for my self	4	1	2
	Pd Mrs Lawson for 3 pair coloured Silk Stockings to my self	2	5	0
Sep[r]	Pd for a pair of Buck Skine Gloves to my self & for Gloves from York	1	8	0
Nov[r]	Pd Mr M[c] ghie in part of my hunters Cloaths, by Cash for Candles pay'd to Mr Fairholme in London p[r] Mr M[c]ghies obligatory letter.	20	0	0
Nov[r]	Pd Mrs Lawson for 2 pair boot Stockings for my self		7	4
	Pd Hercules for making all my Cloaths to the date	5	18	0

Date	Item	£	s	d
Nov^{r}	Pd Mr Hamilton for my new hunters Cloaths	29	18	3
	Pd Mr Scot for a Grey Waistcoat & Linning for my self	1	13	0
	1763 Sume	£70	8	1

Discharge on My Stables Hounds horses Coach &c 1763

Date	Item	£	s	d
Jay^{r} 26	Pd Gardiner ferrier all shoes, attendance, &c to the date & all Drugs & cures to my horses	6	10	0
Feby 16	Pd John Hall for 16 bolls, 8p of old oats delivered in Sepr last	12	8	0
	Pd Lord Galloway for 2 young fillies 4 & 3 year old May last	36	15	0
March	Pd T. Borthwick for Oyle tar hogslard Black & other triffles to ye date		14	11
	Pd Dryden Smith for Decr Jay^{r} & Feby pr disged Acc^{ts}	5	7	4
	Pd for building a division in Carnth Kennell & for the Stones	1	4	0
April 30	Pd T Borthwick for mendings, for Candles &c to the date		6	2
	Pd Thos for attending my Dogs this Season in full		18	0
May 17	Pd for a Mare to carry my Wife	5	0	0
30	Pd Wm Grahame for hoove salve for Candles Combs brushes &c P^{r} disge	2	7	0
	Pd the Cariage of Dogmeal from Leith to Dryden		4	10
	Pd Stodert & Prentice for 4 bolls of Pease to my hunters	2	13	4
	Pd Carlindean(1) tennents, Hugh Smith Wm Kelly Wm Young Ja^{s} Stodert, Wm Spence, John Anderson for 129 bolls 14 Pecks of Corn & Some Straw	115	5	11
June	Pd George Aitken for 21 bolls 8 pecks Corn & Straw	12	10	10
	Pd John Weir for 18 bolls 4 pecks Corn & Straw	10	12	11

June	Pd John Weir & Wm Cochran for Hay Crop 1762	36	17	11
	Pd Dryden Smith for March April & May	3	14	10
	Pd Thos Mitchell for 12 bolls Corn & Straw	7	0	0
July	Pd my Coach & Post Chaise Duty for the year 1763 to April 1764	8	0	0
Augt	Pd Dryden Smith for June & July	2	17	9
Sepr	Pd Dryden Smith for August	3	2	4
14	Pd Wm Grahame for Saddles mending, for phisick for Girths for 3 bolls brawn pr acc to the date	1	16	6
Ocr	Pd Wm Grahames Expences when sent to Coupar races		10	0
	Pd for 2 bolls meal to my young Pointers with Clerk	1	0	0
Novr	Pd Gibson & Inglis for 31 bolls 4 pecks oats sent to my Stables in May & June last	21	12	9
26	Pd for 26 bolls Dog meal to my beagles from their coming to the Kennels to the date	17	10	0
	Pd James Wallace for Smith Work to M 1763	12	18	0
	Pd Lanark Saidler for Bridles & all repairs		12	0
	Pd Carnwath Coupar to the date & Dr Blair for Phisick		4	8
	Pd Andw Smith for horse Drugs & attendance to the date		16	0
	Pd Andw Smith for Litter received last Spring	2	0	0
	Pd Thomas for attending my beagles to Mart last		15	0
	Pd for 22 bolls 8p of oats from George Aitken & John Hall	18	0	0
	Pd Dryden Smith for November & all preceedings	3	5	0
	Pd Wm Grahame for hoove salve & Wm Kelly for triffles	1	12	6
	Pd Pegs expences at Coupar & Wm Patersons accts to the date	5	6	0
	Pd my Coachman for Oyle, repairs, &c to the date		15	1
	Pd Purdie for phisick &c ropes 2 Whips & several triffles	1	11	2

		£	s	d
Novr 26	Pd George Mc Dougal for Drugs & pains with my horses		5	0
	Pd for Candles & Cracklings preceeding Novr from Loanhead	1	13	0
	Pd my Brother for his horse Rodundo	6	0	0
	1763 Sume	£360	13	9[(2)]

Notes

(1) Carlindean is one of the farms on the Carnwath Estate. This entry indicates that enclosure and amalgamation had not reached there yet.

(2) The Laird made an error of £12 here; the correct total is £372.13.9.

Discharge on my Serv^ts Cloaths & Wadges 1763

		£	s	d
Feby 24	Pd the Cobler all repairs by him to the date		5	6
May 29	Pd for new boots to the Postilion & Wm Paterson	1	11	0
	Pd Carnwath Shoemaker all work to the date		10	0
June	Pd George Montgomery in part of his years Wadges	2	0	0
	Pd Wm Montgomery in part of his years Wadges	1	0	0
	Pd Thos Borthwick & Wm Kelly equally in part of their Wadges	4	0	0
	Pd Dryden Taylor in full of all Work to W^y 1763	3	14	9
July	Pd Mr Smart in full of Cloath for my Serv^ts to ye date	9	12	4
	Pd David Wilson in part of his Wadges	4	0	0
	Pd Ja^s Thomson all Leather breatches to my Serv^ts pr disged Acct	6	6	0
Nov^r	Pd Cuthbertson for 40 ells of Grey cloath for Serv^ts frocks	5	6	0
	Pd for new boots to my Coachman & all repairs at Carn^th	1	5	0
	Pd Carnwath Taylor for all repairs		16	4
	Pd Ja^s Clerk & David Sanderson their Wadges to M 1763	1	5	0

Nov[r]	Pd Ja[s] Stodert & all my Serv[ts] Wadges (in Livery) besides £11 pay'd in Summer, & Henry Larche in full to M 1763	85 0 0
	Pd for boots & Buckskine breatches to Daniel Ramsay	1 8 0
	Pd Mrs Lawson for lace to Daniel Ramsays hatt	11 6
	1763 Sume	£128 11 5

Discharge on Messcelanys Building Ditching Gardens &c 1763

March	Pd for a Smoak Guard from Whittinghame	14 0
	Pd Dryden Days Wadges men for Dec[r] Jay[r] & Feb[y]	5 17 4
	Pd for a new ditch to fence the west side of Whitehill farm	2 13 11
April	Pd Clerk for herding Carn[th] Parks from Town hens	3 6
30	Pd the Workmen at Bristow Quarry to the date	1 3 6
	Pd for paint oyle, Ropes, Weights to Carnwath house	19 9
May 17	Pd for filling Dung Carts, Weeding & Stoneing 8 Acres of Byre Flatts	2 4 8
	Pd George Bean for 5 new padlocks & many Jobs	3 4 0
	Pd W[m] Spence for Gates & many other repairs	2 18 6
	Pd for a bull for my grassing Cows at Carnwath	2 18 0
	Pd for 209 loads of Coals & Cariage Ale	3 0 11
	Pd for planting at Carnwath under Tho[s] Sinclair	3 9 8
	Pd for Dunghills & Spreading last Winter & for some not yet	2 17 9
	Pd Mr Welsh for 36 bolls, 8 pecks, Seed Oats for Carnwath	27 7 6
June	Pd Tho[s] Sinclair for Ropes, Tar, Custome, &c &c	2 10 8
	Pd Alex[r] Broun for grinding to the date	13 4
	Pd for trenching Dryden low banks for potatoes	1 14 8

		£	s	d
June	Pd Ja^{s} Monylas for sawing timber & all work at Dryden	2	19	8
	Pd for new Tubs to Dryden Gardings	1	4	2
	Pd Chrighton for upholding Dryden Windows to W^{y} 1763	1	10	0
	Pd all Days Wadges Work at Dryden to the date	4	11	4
	Pd Wm Miller for Garden Seeds, for Clover, for Spads Syths, Knives p^{r} dischged Acc^{t} from W^{y} 1756 to Whity 1763	63	18	0
	Pd for winning Stones at Bristow Quarry		16	0
	Pd for digging Clay for Bricks at Carnwath		15	0
	Pd Lanark Glasier all work at Carnwath house (potty &c &c)	1	2	0
Nov^{r}	Pd for 154 bolls of Lime & Cariage for park Walls Dung Hill houses &c at Carnwath	6	0	0
	Pd Ja^{s} Paterson for nails Iron Tar Candle &c	2	8	0
	Pd Wm Walker all Cariages to the date	1	1	0
	Pd Wm Spence for Roofing my Serv^{ts} room & all other work	5	9	0
	Pd Lanark Sclater[1] for the Serv^{ts} room & Carnth house to M 1763	2	4	0
	Pd Lanark Glasier for new Windows & all repairs	1	9	0
	Pd for 266 load of Coals & Cariage Ale to Tennents	3	17	0
	Pd for 5 sacks & 2 new Girnal[2] Sives	1	6	0
	Pd for Shearing & Inning my Crop at Carnwath	12	1	0
	Pd for Jobs & all hired Days Wadges Men at Carnwath	10	16	0
	Pd Andrew Somerville & 4 other men for filling up Peet holes, & making Watter runs, &c in Carnwath parks	3	19	0
	Pd for Nails to my new house & to the Gadgers house	2	0	0
	Pd for butter to Carnwath Carts (?)		8	6
	Pd George Baine for repairs & many triffles & New Work	3	18	6
	Pd my 5 Work Serv^{ts} at Carnwath their Wadges to m 1763	15	3	4

Nov^r	Pd Thos Sinclair for Ropes Customes Turnpikes Tar &c &c	3	10	6
	Pd all Work at Hay Ferns &c at Dryden to Day Labourers	7	18	8
	Pd my Gardiner for thorn haughs bought for me	2	17	1
	Pd Ja^s Monylas in full of all Work	1	14	4
	Pd Thos Mitchell for new Cart Wheels &c	1	8	9
	Pd John Lockhart for Sawing fire Wood	1	10	0
	Pd Miles & Ritchardson for 62 bolls of Lime	3	8	10
	Pd Thos Sinclair & 4 Work Serv^ts their Wadges to M 1763	20	0	0
	Pd my Gardiner & 3 Lads to Mart^s 1763 all Wadges	11	0	0
	Pd Wm Grahame & 5 Work Serv^ts their meal at Carn^th	26	10	1
	Pd for Bread to Tennents Serv^ts &c	3	1	0
	Pd Dryden Gardiner & 3 Lads Meal to M 1763	18	17	1
1763	Discharge on my Work Servants meal at Dryden & Thos Sinclair to M 1763	25	3	9
	1763 Sume	£340	4	3(3)

Notes

(1) Sclater—Slater.

(2) The Girnal was the Storehouse where the grain collected as rent was kept.

(3) The Laird has made an error of four shillings; the correct total should be £340.8.3.

Discharge on Meall Malt Rum Wine Plate 1763

Feby 4	Pd Mr. Menzies for Rum brandy &c	3	4	6
	Pd for Sugar & leamons to make Shrub	3	9	0
June 2	Pd Ja^s Stodert for Strong & Small bear to my Carn^th family	10	16	6
	Pd Weir & Cochrane for 40 bolls barley for malt to Dryden	28	10	0
	Pd D^d Haig for making 56 bolls barley into malt for excise duty for Do. for ale furnished to Dryden this spring	11	16	7

June 2	Pd Mr. Hume for 2 Hog^ds of Claret for bottles Corks &c[(1)] pr Disge	48	0	0
	Pd the tax on my Plate to Jully 5 1764	2	15	0
	Pd James Stodert all Ale furnished to Carnwath to M 1763	11	16	0
	Pd for 17 bolls Meal to my family at Carnwath	13	3	6
	Pd for 60 bolls 10 pecks of meal from Old Custom & Carnwath to my Family at Dryden[(2)]	46	19	8
	Pd Mr. Blackwood for 41 Gallons of Rum & a hog^d of White Wine bottles, Corks, &c pr Acct discharged	36	17	6
	1763 Sume	£127	8	3[(3)]

My acct^s end here for 1763

Notes

(1) The Laird bought a hogshead of claret and bottled it at home. This was quite common practice until the beginning of the 20th century.

(2) Old Custom was probably the Custom House. Carnwath as the larger Estate produced more corn and meal in the form of rent, and the surplus had to be transported to Dryden for consumption.

(3) It looks as though the pounds had been transposed from 217 to 127.

Discharge on pocket mony 1764

Jay^r	Pd for 16 Tickets to the Accademy	3	3	0
	Pd my yearly pay^t to the Hunters for 1764 & also for being absent from Coupar meeting last year	10	10	0
10	Spent at our Election (in Walkers) for preses &c	1	4	0
Feb^y	Pd for 16 tickets to the Accademy	2	16	0
	Pd for a cage to my Wife's parrot in a present to her	1	1	0
	Pd Mr Wilson for Chairs & Stools a present to Mrs Lawson	3	7	0
	Pd for a Chaise to Dalkeith maintenance &c		6	0
	Given to the Collection for the Infirmary	1	1	0
	Pd Peter Dudgeon for 2 deer	1	10	0

Feby	Spent in my pocket mony at Plays, Races, Assemblys Concerts Taverns for Cards &c &c during the Winter	30	0	0
March	Pd at clearing with the Royal Bank		5	0
	Pd Mr Rae for tying my teeth &c		15	0
April	Spent for eatables at Carnwath to the date	1	12	6
	Pd for Drink(1) catching 2 bucks at Hamilton		6	0
	Pd Mr Birnell for all London newspapers to the date	4	5	0
May 21	Pd my expences at Linton 2 different times		14	0
	Pd for Boardwadges at Edinr Breakfast & a pair of Spurs		14	4
	Given in a present to help John Stodert & for his Journy to London	20	0	0
	Pd for upholding Carnwath fishing nett to Wy 1764		15	0
	Pd for keeping Carnwath clock in order to Do 1764		2	6
	Pd the Rent of some poor peoples houses	1	8	4
	Pd Alexr Broun abatement for the turnpike road to Wy 1764		10	0
June 15	Pd for eatables at Carnwath		9	6

Note

(1) Two words indecipherable.

1764	**Discharge on Stables Hounds Horses Coach &c**			
Feby	Pd Mr Lock 32 bolls of Dog meal furnished Feby 1762 for Carnwath	23	9	4
	Pd for 32 bolls Dog meal from Dalkeith market for Dryden	18	2	8
	Pd Dryden Smith for Decr & Jayr	3	4	8
	Pd Cleland for a new Servts Saddle & many repairs	1	16	0
	Pd Mr Crichton for all Wheels harness Coach work &c pr Disge	13	5	0
	Pd for Cloath Embroidery & mounting, to 2 new Servts housings	2	19	5
	Pd Johnston for a Coach horse	18	0	0
	Pd Mr Lumisdean for Mr Cunninghams horse Figure with Saddle & Cloaths &c	54	18	0

			£	s	d
March 7	Pd for 11 bolls of oats to my horses in Edin^r		5	18	9
13	Pd Riddell Farier for Drugs & Shoes attendance &c		3	0	0
	Pd for a boll & half of Oats to Bristow house Stables			15	0
April	Pd Dryden Smith for Feb^y & March		3	9	9
	Pd for 3 bolls of oats to my horses at Edin^r		1	13	9
	Pd all expences in recovering Tiger at Edin^r & for his Collar & Chain		1	7	0
	Pd for 4 bolls of Dog meal to Carnwath		2	6	6
	Pd for repairing the 2 Wheeled Chair, harness &c		3	0	0
	Pd Wm Grahame for brushes brawn Phisick hoove Salve &c		2	5	0
June 1	Pd George Aitken for 73 bolls oats & fodder £40.15.8. Pd John Weir for 31 bolls of oats & strae £17.14.4.		58	10	0
	Pd John Weir for hay crop 1763	£15			
	Pd Wm Cochrane for hay crop 1763	£42			
	Pd David Wilson for hay crop 1762	£26.5	83	5	0
	Pd Dryden Smith for April & May		2	10	0
	Pd Mitchell for ten bolls of corn & straw		5	16	8
	Pd Thos Jackson all attendance on my Dogs this season			13	6

		£	s	d
1764	**Discharge on Misselanys building planting Labouring Gardings, Work Servants &c**			
Jay^r	Pd James Cleland a small accompt per disge to the date		12	6
	Pd Mr Rainnie my acc^t for Iron to the date	13	6	10
	Pd Mr Jamison all Work to Bristow house & offices		17	0
	Pd Bell & Milne for wright work to Bristow house		13	10
	Pd Mr Wilson all Wright work to Bristow house & gate pr Disge	7	14	8
March	Pd for 27 Standing Trees left in the Lee wood & haughs	7	0	0
	Pd Dryden Timber Sawyers to acc^t	2	0	0
	Pd Baillie Wilson in full for all timber to Carnwath & Bristow house & several small articles p^r disged acct in full	21	14	9

Month	Day	Entry	£	s	d
March		Pd for 2 fire Skreens to Carnwath & Bristow house		8	0
May		Pd Carnwath massons for 2 floors, laid hardened & smoothed by them		11	0
	28	Pd Hugh Lows Wadges from Marts to Whity 1764	1	0	0
		Pd Andw Rait pr advance of his Wadges	3	0	0
		Pd for a pair of little wheels for a Cart (unshod)		16	8
		Pd for 190 loads of Coals & Cariage Ale	2	15	5
		Pd for 150 bolls of lime & Cariage to Carnwath parks	5	12	6
		Pd for Dunghills bought to my Parks at Carnwath	3	15	10
June	1	Pd Ramsay Brown Gilbert Penman Crawford Penman all Days Wadges in Carnwath parks to ye date	8	16	8
		Pd for thatching the Gardiner & Gadgers houses		12	0
		Pd for ane Inner Ditch in the fold park	2	2	6
		Pd for the Ditch from the Stone dike to the moss band Draine	2	0	0
		Pd for the Ditch to Carlindean Gate from Jas Crawfords Gate	3	2	4
		Pd my Ditchers to account of Drains	4	0	0
		Pd my Ditchers for the Draine at the moss band Gate		12	6
		Pd Carnwath Massons to acct per advance on Quarrie Work	4	0	0
		Pd Wm Spence for a Cart & all Wright work Pr disge	3	9	8
		Pd Carnwath Glasier all work to the date		13	5
	4	Pd for new Glass Windows to Dryden house hot beds &c	1	9	6
		Pd for Dryden Windows to Wy 1764 pr contract	1	10	0
		Pd all Days Wadges at Dryden to the date	3	18	0
		Pd Thos Sinclair in full for tar Custome Oyle expences &c	2	11	6
		Pd Alexr Brown all moutars(1) to the date		5	0
		Pd James Borthwick for Potatoe Seed		15	0
		Pd Mr Gordon bookseller in full of postages books paper &c per his disged acct in full	9	4	9

June 4	Pd Robt Linds Wife all herding to ye date	1 10 0
	Pd Mungo Watson for a boll of early seed oats	10 6
	Pd John Stodert all Custome for Carts, expences of work &c	9 6

Note

(1) Moutar—multure; the payment to the miller for grinding corn.

Discharge on my Cloaths 1764
No Entry

Discharge on Servants Wadges & Liverys 1764

Jay[r]	Pd Thos[s] Black to Marts[s] 1763	15 0 0
	Pd James Clerk in advance of Wadges	9 6
	Pd Ogilve for buckskine breatches furnished to a footman in 1760	1 5 0
May 31	Pd Carnwath Shoemaker for boots to the postilion & all repairs	1 10 4
June 6	Pd Dryden Taylor all work to y[e] date p[r] disged acc[t]	2 8 0
	Pd Jas Purdie W[m] Kelly & Tho[s] Borthwick each £2 in advance of their years Wadges due Marts 1764	6 0 0
	Pd Daniel Ramsay & D[d] Wilson each £3 in part of Wadges due M 1764	6 0 0

Discharge on Rum Wine Plate Meal Malt &c 1764

	Pd Mr Ross all Wine & Rum p[r] discharged Acc[t]		10 9 0
June 1	Pd James Stodert for all Ale to Carnwath house		7 14 0
	Pd James Stodert for six bolls of malt & ten pints spirits sent to Dryden		6 2 0
	Pd John Weir for 7 bolls of barley for malt to Dryden	£4.14.6	
	Pd W[m] Cochran for 5 bolls four pecks barley for D[o]	£3.10.10	8 5 4
6	Pd Mr Hunter all Strong Ale furnished to me p[r] disged Acct		10 1 0
	Pd Pringle & Haig all Ale & for malting to y[e] date p[r] disge		10 5 0

Discharge on my Cloaths 1764[1]

March 14	Pd Thomsons Widdow for two bob Wigs & Several triffles	2 12 6

Note

(1) The Laird died on October 30th 1764 so this year's accounts are incomplete.

THE END